MW01194687

101 THINGS COLLEGE STUDENTS SHOULD KNOW

From Navigating Academics, Campus Life, Budgeting, Career Planning, Life Skills, Health, and Much More!

PETER MYERS

ISBN: 978-1-962496-14-8

For questions, please reach out to <u>Support@OakHarborPress.com</u>

Please consider leaving a review!

Just visit: OakHarborPress.com/Reviews

Copyright 2024. Oak Harbor Press. All Rights Reserved.

No part of this book may be reproduced or transmitted in any form or by any means, electronic or mechanical, including photocopying, recording, or by any other form without written permission from the publisher.

FREE BONUS

SCAN TO GET OUR NEXT
BOOK FOR FREE!

TABLE OF CONTENTS

INTRODUCTION

Welcome to the exhilarating odyssey of higher education — a journey that marks the transition from the familiar corridors of high school to the uncharted territories of college life. Whether you're a wide-eyed freshman or a seasoned upperclassman, this is your personal invitation to embark on a transformative experience that goes far beyond textbooks and lecture halls. The next few years will be a whirlwind of challenges, triumphs, and self-discovery, and we're here to be your compass, guiding you through the labyrinth of academia and beyond.

The transition from high school to college is a monumental leap, one that often feels like crossing a threshold into an entirely new dimension. Suddenly, you're faced with a myriad of choices, responsibilities, and freedoms that can feel both liberating and overwhelming. As you go through this transitional period, it's important to recognize that you're not alone. Each student grapples with unique challenges, and it's perfectly normal to feel a mix of excitement, uncertainty, and curiosity.

This book is more than just a guide; it's a companion for your academic and personal journey. Throughout these pages, you'll find wisdom distilled from the collective experiences of those who have walked the path before you — insights that span the spectrum from academic success to personal well-being. Consider this book your survival kit, equipped with tools to tackle challenges, capitalize on opportunities, and make the most of this extraordinary chapter in your life.

Academia is not merely a battleground for grades, but a playground for intellectual exploration. From navigating the complexities of your course load to discovering your passion, each moment presents an opportunity. As you dive into your chosen field of study, take a moment to appreciate the process of learning itself. Embrace the uncertainties, ask questions, and savor the thrill of expanding your intellectual horizons.

Beyond the classroom, you'll find yourself immersed in a vibrant tapestry of campus life. Friendships, extracurricular activities, and the occasional existential crisis are all part of the rich mosaic that defines your college experience. This book will offer guidance on balancing academic demands with social and personal development, ensuring that you emerge not only with a degree, but as a well-rounded individual, ready to face the challenges of the professional world.

However, your journey doesn't end with graduation; it's merely a step towards the next chapter of your life. When you dive into the professional world, armed with your degree and experiences, the transition can be just as daunting as entering college. This guide is designed to be a companion throughout your entire academic journey, providing insights into the professional landscape, job hunting strategies, and tips for thriving in the workplace.

To students on the cusp of a new academic adventure, this is your guidebook for the odyssey ahead. Embrace challenges, relish victories, and remember that every stumble is part of the path to success.

CHAPTER ONE: ACADEMIC SUCCESS

Unlocking academic success in college can seem all-consuming and stressful. Fortunately, millions of people have successfully conquered college, paving the way for you. Read on for key insights that'll elevate your learning journey and set you on the path to triumph in your college pursuits.

[1]
TIME MANAGEMENT TECHNIQUES

Managing your time effectively is critical in the hectic world of academia. Let's dive into some time management techniques that will help you conquer your coursework—and still have time for some well-deserved fun.

First things first: creating a schedule. Use a planner, digital app, or even a simple to-do list to organize your tasks. Break down big assignments into smaller, manageable chunks. This will not only make them less overwhelming, but also help you keep track of your progress.

Prioritize tasks based on due date and importance. Tackling urgent assignments first ensures you meet deadlines, while focusing on high-priority tasks keeps you on top of your game. Learn to say "no" to unnecessary commitments that can drain your time and energy.

Embrace the concept of time blocking. Assign specific blocks of time to different activities—whether it's studying, socializing, or self-care. This will help you maintain focus and prevent burnout.

Time-blocking also allows you to practice the art of batch-processing. Instead of randomly jumping between tasks, group similar activities together and tackle them in quick succession. This minimizes the mental energy needed for context-switching and allows you to dive deep into each task more efficiently.

Procrastination is the enemy, but you can break the cycle by starting with small, manageable steps. Set short breaks during study sessions to keep your mind fresh and avoid burnout.

Finally, don't forget to schedule downtime. Taking breaks and getting enough sleep are crucial for maintaining your overall well-being.

[2]
EFFECTIVE STUDY HABITS

Developing good study habits will help you get the grades you need to succeed. It will take practice and experimentation to find the best fit for you, but putting the time in to build a routine will relieve a lot of stress in the long run. This section provides a glimpse at some effective study habits that will help you conquer your coursework and emerge victorious.

First off, find your study sanctuary. Whether it's a cozy corner in the library, a coffee shop, or your bedroom desk, having a dedicated study space boosts focus and productivity. Make it comfortable and free from distractions — this is your academic dojo.

Ever heard of the Pomodoro Technique? It's a game-changer. Break your study time into 25-minute chunks, followed by a 5-minute break. After four rounds, take a longer break. This not only keeps your mind sharp but also prevents fatigue.

You can also give the Feynman Technique a try. Go over what you've learned as if you're explaining it to someone else. If you can simplify and communicate complex concepts, you've truly mastered the material.

Active learning is your secret weapon. Instead of passively reading or highlighting, engage with the material. Summarize key points in your own words, teach the concepts to an imaginary audience, or create flashcards. The more actively you participate, the better you'll retain information.

Variety is the spice of study life. Mix up your subjects and topics to keep things interesting. Monotony can lead to boredom and reduced retention. Rotate between subjects to keep your brain engaged and alert.

In addition, diversifying how you learn the information helps it stick. Instead of just reading your textbook, go online and find additional videos and learning material. The more exposure you have to the concepts, the better you'll understand them.

Team up with study buddies. Collaborative learning not only makes studying more enjoyable, but also provides different perspectives on the material. Just make sure the group remains focused — it's not a social gathering!

Embrace the power of self-discipline. Set realistic goals, create a schedule, and stick to them. Discipline is the key to consistent progress. There are many study techniques out there, so it's important to take some time to research and try out different methods to find what works best for you.

[3]
NAVIGATING ONLINE RESOURCES

The vast array of online resources might seem daunting, but fear not — this book is here to guide you through mastering these tools for your college journey. Let's embark on the adventure of navigating the digital realm to enhance your academic experience.

Firstly, you must learn to discern *reliable* sources. Not all websites are created equal. Stick to reputable platforms, educational institutions, and peer-reviewed articles. Check for citations and look into the author's credentials to ensure credibility.

Master the art of search engines. Utilize advanced search operators to refine your results. Experiment with quotation marks, site-specific searches, and filters. *Google* isn't just a search engine; it's a powerful research ally.

Organize your findings like a pro. Use bookmark folders, citation management tools, or note-taking apps to keep track of valuable resources. This not only saves time, but also makes it easier to revisit crucial information.

Explore online databases offered by your college library. These treasure troves house a wealth of scholarly articles, journals, and research papers. Get familiar with databases like *JSTOR*, *PubMed*, or *IEEE Xplore* — they're mines containing academic gems.

Embrace the wealth of online courses and tutorials. Platforms like *Coursera*, *Khan Academy*, and *edX* offer a plethora of courses to complement your studies. Whether it's brushing up on a challenging topic or diving into a new skill, these resources act as your academic sidekicks.

Collaborate through virtual platforms. Connect with classmates on discussion forums, virtual study groups, or collaborative documents. Platforms like *Google Drive*, *Microsoft Teams*, and *Slack* facilitate seamless teamwork, even in the digital realm.

Stay tech-savvy. Familiarize yourself with productivity tools like *Microsoft Office 365*, *Google Workspace*, and *Notion*. Efficiently manage documents, collaborate with peers, and stay organized with these digital powerhouses.

[4]
WRITING
RESEARCH PAPERS

Crafting a stellar research paper is a rite of passage in college, and we're here to share some valuable tips to help you ace this academic endeavor. When you write a compelling research paper, you'll not only impress your professors, but you'll also have the opportunity to contribute meaningfully to your field of study.

To begin with, choose your topic wisely. Select something you're genuinely interested in — it makes the entire process more engaging and fulfilling. Ensure your topic is specific enough to explore deeply, but broad enough to find ample resources.

Conduct thorough research. Dive into academic databases, journals, and reputable sources related to your subject. Take organized notes and keep track of your sources from the get-go. This initial groundwork will form your paper's strong foundation.

Craft a killer thesis statement. This is the backbone of your paper, summarizing your main argument or topic of research. You should draft this first so you can continue to tweak it throughout the writing process. Make it clear, concise, and thought-provoking. It's the roadmap that guides both you and your readers through the paper.

Outline like a pro—structure is key. Create a plan for your paper, breaking it down into sections and subsections. This will keep your thoughts organized while ensuring a logical flow from introduction to conclusion. Each paragraph should have a topic sentence, a supporting fact (quote or summarized research), an analysis in your own words, and a transition sentence into the next point.

It should look something like this:

1. Introduction
   a. Topic of paper
   b. Introduction of historical background
   c. Key terms for understanding the paper
   d. Thesis statement
2. Key point one (your topic sentence)
   a. Quote or data
   b. Analysis
   c. Transition
3. Key point two (your topic sentence)
   a. Quote or data
   b. Analysis
   c. Transition
4. Key point three (your topic sentence)
   a. Quote or data
   b. Analysis
   c. Transition
5. Conclusion
   a. Summary the meaning of the paper
   b. What is the big world picture?
   c. How do you think it relates to the world?

Once you've figured out your initial points, go ahead and start drafting sentences, right into the outline. Enter quotes or statistics into their proper places first. Then, describe your interpretation of what it means. It's easiest to leave transitions and topic sentences for last. Once each line has a complete sentence, the bulk of your first draft will be complete.

Write with clarity and precision. Academic writing can be dense, but it's crucial to be as plain as possible. Avoid unnecessary jargon, use concise language, and explain complex ideas in a straightforward manner.

Cite your sources diligently. Plagiarism is a serious offense! Familiarize yourself with the citation style required by your professor — whether it's APA, MLA, or Chicago — and apply it consistently throughout your paper.

Edit and revise relentlessly. Your first draft is just the beginning — there's a reason it's called a "rough" draft! Go through multiple rounds of editing, checking for coherence, grammar, and style. Better yet, have a peer or mentor review your work for a fresh perspective.

[5]
PREPARING FOR EXAMS

Preparing for exams is generally stressful. It's impossible to know for sure if you'll get the grade you want, but good preparation can dramatically increase your chance of acing an exam. Here are some battle-tested strategies to help you conquer your exams like a true academic gladiator.

First, create a study plan. Break down your material into manageable sections and allocate specific time slots for each. A well-organized plan reduces stress and ensures comprehensive coverage of the syllabus.

Prioritize your study material. Identify key concepts, focus on challenging topics, and allocate more time to areas that need extra attention. Not all topics are created equal, so know where to invest your energy for maximum impact.

As with studying, embrace active learning. Instead of passively reading notes, engage with the material. Practice with flashcards, teach concepts to a study buddy, and solve practice questions.

In addition to participating in study groups, you can seek out additional tutoring. Most colleges offer specific hours when a tutor is present. Find these and make use of them, even if you feel comfortable with the material. A tutor will be able to help you understand it better and help you prepare for the exam.

Optimize your study environment. Find a quiet, comfortable space with minimal distractions. Ensure good lighting and keep your study materials organized. Your environment sets the tone for productive study sessions.

Take strategic breaks. Your brain needs time to absorb information. Schedule short breaks during study sessions to recharge. Use techniques like the Pomodoro method—study for focused intervals and take short breaks to maintain peak concentration.

Practice past exams or sample questions. Familiarize yourself with the exam format and types of questions you might encounter. This not only boosts confidence, but also helps you manage time effectively during the actual exam.

Finally, manage exam stress. It's normal to feel a bit anxious, but excess stress can hinder performance. Practice relaxation techniques like deep breathing or meditation to keep stress at bay.

[6]
CHOOSING A MAJOR

Choosing a major is a significant decision. It's normal for students to change their major multiple times throughout their college career.

Self-reflection is key. Take a moment to assess your interests, passions, and strengths. What subjects make you curious? What activities make you lose track of time? Online aptitude tests are available to help you identify the type of work that best suits your personality. Identifying these strengths can provide valuable insights into potential majors.

Explore, explore, explore! College is the perfect time to dip your toes into different subjects. Take diverse courses, attend workshops, and engage in extracurricular activities. This hands-on approach allows you to experience various fields and make an informed decision.

Consider your long-term goals. Think about the kind of career you envision for yourself. Research potential job markets, salary expectations, and growth opportunities related to different majors. Aligning your major with your career goals ensures a smoother transition post-graduation.

Talk to professionals in each field. Reach out to professors, career counselors, and professionals working in your areas of interest. Their advice can give you valuable insights into the practical aspects of different majors.

Don't be afraid to pivot. It's okay to change your major if you realize your initial choice isn't the right fit. College is a time of discovery, and your interests may evolve over time. Embrace flexibility to find your true passion.

Consider the interdisciplinary approach. Some majors blend various disciplines, offering a holistic view of a subject. If you find it challenging to narrow down your interests, explore interdisciplinary majors that allow you to develop multiple subjects at once.

[7]
SEEKING
ACADEMIC HELP

At one time or another, every college student hits a point where the textbooks start looking like cryptic codes, and that's completely normal. Seeking academic help is not a sign of weakness; it's a smart move.

Before you can ask for help, know what resources are available to you. Colleges offer a wide variety of support services, from tutoring centers to writing labs. Familiarize yourself with these havens of knowledge and make them your go-to spots when the academic seas get rough.

Don't hesitate to ask questions in class. Your professors are there to help you understand the material. If something isn't clicking, raise your hand, shoot them an email, or visit during office hours.

Form study groups. Collaborative learning is a valuable resource. Team up with classmates to dissect challenging topics, solve problems, and share insights. Everyone brings a unique perspective, creating a rich learning environment.

Consider peer tutoring. Sometimes, learning from a fellow student can be a game-changer, and teaching someone else can help you internalize key concepts. Many colleges have peer tutoring programs where students who excel in a subject can help others navigate the academic terrain.

Writing centers are your secret weapon. Crafting essays and research papers can be daunting, but writing centers exist to guide you. They can help with everything from brainstorming ideas to fine-tuning your prose.

Visit the academic advising office. These wizards of academia can assist in charting your academic path, selecting courses, and ensuring you're on the right track.

[8]
PARTICIPATING IN CLASS DISCUSSIONS

Class discussions aren't just a chance make it through another course; they're your ticket to deeper understanding and meaningful engagement. You'll want to have some strategies in your back pocket so you can make your presence felt and your contributions count during lively class discussions.

As with everything, come prepared. Stay on top of reading, assignments, and any other materials before class. This groundwork sets the stage for active participation and ensures you can contribute meaningfully to the conversation.

Listen actively. When your classmates are speaking, don't just plan your response. Truly listen, absorb their points, and build upon them. This not only enriches the discussion, but also shows respect for your peers' perspectives.

Speak up early and often. Don't wait for the perfect moment; seize it. Share your thoughts, ask questions, and contribute to the dialogue in a concise manner. Your insights matter, and the more you participate, the more you'll get out of the discussion.

Don't fear disagreement. Healthy debates fuel intellectual growth. If you disagree with a point, express your thoughts respectfully. Constructive arguments can lead to a more nuanced understanding of the topic.

[9]
UNDERSTANDING ACADEMIC INTEGRITY

Now we're going to discuss a crucial aspect of your academic journey — maintaining academic integrity. This isn't just about following rules; it's about building a foundation of trust and credibility in your educational pursuits.

Avoid plagiarism like the plague. It's not just copying and pasting; it includes using someone else's ideas, words, or even structure without proper attribution. Always cite your sources and give credit where credit is due.

Collaborate responsibly. Group projects are great opportunities for teamwork, but it's crucial to contribute your fair share. Clearly define individual responsibilities and ensure that everyone is pulling their weight.

Guard your work like a precious gem. Be cautious about sharing your assignments, papers, or exam answers. What might seem like harmless assistance can lead to unintentional violations. It's your responsibility to ensure the integrity of your academic contributions.

Report violations when necessary. If you come across instances of academic dishonesty, don't turn a blind eye.

[10]
LEVERAGING OFFICE HOURS

Professors' office hours are important. Not only do these offer an opportunity to clarify expectations for your class, but they also build a personal rapport with your professor. The first time you visit, it might feel awkward; however, the more often you go, the more you can get out of the experience. Let's explore how you can make the most of this valuable resource to enhance your learning journey.

Overcome the hesitation. It's common to feel a bit intimidated, but remember, professors are there to help you succeed. Office hours are also a good opportunity to let your professors know what your life looks like outside of the classroom. If they understand what pressures you are under, they will help you where they can.

Come prepared. Before attending office hours, review your notes, assignments, or any specific questions you have. Respect your time—and your professor's—by being organized.

Ask for clarification on feedback. If you have a question about graded assignments or exams, don't hesitate to go over the feedback during office hours, seeking clarification on comments or suggestions.

Discuss your academic goals. Use office hours to communicate your academic aspirations, career goals, or potential areas of interest within the subject. Professors often have valuable insights and can offer guidance on courses, research opportunities, and career paths aligned with your interests.

Build relationships. Establishing a bond with your professors can be beneficial beyond the current course. It can lead to mentorship opportunities, letters of recommendation, and insights into their field. Take the opportunity to connect on a personal level, demonstrating your commitment to your education.

Keep in mind that office hours are not just for struggling students— they're for anyone aiming to excel. Don't underestimate the power of these one-on-one interactions; they can be transformative for your academic journey.

CHAPTER TWO:
CAMPUS LIFE

From classes to clubs, friendships to fun, campus life is what you'll be living for the next few years. Get ready to embrace diversity, navigate new experiences, and discover your own path. These ten parts of campus just scratch the surface, but they'll help prepare you for an ideal college experience.

[11]
DORM LIVING ESSENTIALS

As you gear up for the exciting new chapter called college, it's crucial to make your dorm room feel like home. Here are some essentials to ensure your space is more than just a crash pad.

First things first—bedding! Invest in quality sheets, a cozy comforter, and an assortment of pillows. A good night's sleep is your secret weapon to conquering those early-morning classes. Next up, storage solutions. Think under-bed organizers, storage cubes, and hooks. Maximize that limited space like the organizational superhero you are.

Lighting is another important aspect in creating the right atmosphere. Grab a desk lamp for late-night study sessions. Strip LED or fairy lights can help create an atmosphere that makes you feel comfortable. Power strips are your trusty utility belts, ensuring all your gadgets stay charged and ready for action.

No fortress is complete without a study zone, so equip yourself with the essentials: a reliable laptop, notebooks, and pens. A comfortable desk chair will be your throne as you conquer assignments and projects. Don't forget noise-canceling headphones for when the outside world invades your solitude.

Now, let's talk about sustenance. A mini-fridge and microwave combo will be your sidekick in the battle against hunger. Stock up on healthy snacks and easy-to-make meals. A coffee maker can also be a valuable ally during those caffeine-fueled study nights.

Finally, add some personal touches. Bring posters, pictures, and items that reflect your personality. Your dorm room is your canvas — decorate it with your unique flair.

[12]
ENGAGING IN STUDENT ORGANIZATIONS

College isn't just about hitting the books; it's a golden opportunity to connect, grow, and make a lasting impact. One of the best ways to do this is by diving into the world of student organizations. Here's a guide to finding and engaging in these incredible communities.

Explore campus resources and check out the student affairs or activities office; they'll have loads of information on various organizations. Attend orientation events or club fairs to get a sense of what you're passionate about and get a taste of the diverse student groups on campus.

Online platforms are your virtual allies. Many colleges have websites or social media pages dedicated to student organizations. Join campus-specific groups on social platforms — it's a great way to stay updated on events, meetings, and opportunities to get involved.

Networking is also a valuable tool. Engage with current members, ask questions, and attend events hosted by organizations you're interested in. Many groups host socials or informational sessions where you can connect with like-minded individuals.

Commitment is key. Once you've found the perfect fit, don't hesitate to join! Participating as an active member will not only enrich your college experience, but also help you build valuable skills and friendships. Attend regular meetings, participate in events, and consider taking on leadership roles.

[13]
CAMPUS
SAFETY TIPS

Your college campus is your new playground, but it's essential to stay safe and aware. Here's a crash course in staying secure while having a blast on campus.

Be aware of your surroundings. Whether you're strolling through the quad or heading to a late-night study session, stay vigilant. Keep in mind the locations of emergency phones and campus security hubs.

If allowed at your school, invest in a good lock for your dorm room. It's your fortress, and a sturdy lock is your first line of defense against uninvited guests. When outside of your room, keep an eye on your stuff in public places. Always lock up when you leave, even if it's just for a quick coffee run.

Buddy up! There's strength in numbers, so try not to venture out alone, especially at night. Whether you're going for a jog, hitting the library, or exploring the town, having a buddy reduces your vulnerability.

Embrace technology for your safety. Download campus safety apps that provide quick access to emergency services, offer virtual escort features, and keep you informed about potential risks on campus.

Know your emergency exits. Whether you're in class, the library, or a dorm building, familiarize yourself with exit routes. In case of a fire or any other emergency, having a plan can make all the difference.

Above all, trust your instincts. If you feel unsafe, don't hesitate to remove yourself from the situation. Your gut is a powerful ally, so listen to it.

[14]
NAVIGATING CAMPUS SERVICES

To get a feel for what services are available to you, the first step is to become familiar with your campus. Take a tour or explore on your own. Locate key spots like the library, student center, health center, cafeteria, and academic advising offices. Knowing where these places are will save you time and make your college life smoother.

Your academic advisor is your ally. Schedule a meeting to discuss your major, class schedule, and any concerns you may have. They're there to guide you through your academic journey and help you stay on track.

The library is more than just a place to find books; it's a treasure trove of resources. Familiarize yourself with research databases, quiet study areas, and librarians who are ready to assist you. The library is your academic haven.

Visit the career center early on to explore potential career paths, get help crafting your resume, and even practice interview skills. They're your guides to post-college success.

Health and wellness should be a priority. Know where the health center is, understand your health insurance, and utilize counseling services if needed. A healthy body and mind are both crucial for a successful college experience.

[15]
BALANCING SOCIAL AND ACADEMIC LIFE

Balancing your social life and academic responsibilities might feel like walking a tightrope, but don't worry—we've got some tips to help you master the art of equilibrium.

First, let's talk about time management. Plan your schedule wisely, create to-do lists, and prioritize tasks. Allocate specific time slots for studying, classes, and social activities. A well-organized calendar is key in maintaining balance.

Set realistic goals. Understand your academic workload and commitments before diving into social activities. FOMO (fear of missing out) is real, but sometimes saying "no" to a social event is necessary to meet academic deadlines or get some much-needed rest.

Create a study routine that works for you. Whether you're an early bird or a night owl, find your prime study time. Consistency is key — establish a routine that aligns with your energy levels and helps you stay focused.

Use study groups wisely. Joining study groups can be an excellent way to socialize while getting work done. Choose groups that are focused and productive, ensuring you benefit academically.

Balance doesn't mean isolation. Cultivate a support system with friends and mentors who understand the importance of both academics and social life. Surround yourself with like-minded individuals who encourage your success.

Practice self-care. Balancing social and academic life is impossible without taking care of yourself. Ensure you get enough sleep, eat well, exercise, and take breaks when needed. A healthy mind and body contribute to overall success.

[16]
DEALING WITH ROOMMATES

Living with someone new is an exciting part of the college experience, but it can also be a challenge, especially if you've never shared a room with someone else before. Luckily, we've got some tips to help you navigate this adventure and create a harmonious living space.

Communication is key, and honesty is your best policy. Start by setting expectations early on. Discuss your daily routines, study habits, and any preferences you may have. Respect personal space and be open about your boundaries.

Establish clear guidelines for shared spaces. Whether it's cleaning schedules, grocery shopping, or bathroom usage, having agreed-upon rules prevents potential conflicts. Write these down if needed — a roommate agreement can be a lifesaver.

Address issues head-on, but with tact. If something bothers you, don't let it simmer! Approach your roommate with a calm and open mind. Use "I" statements to express your feelings and avoid placing blame. Most conflicts can be resolved through open communication.

Be flexible and compromising. Living with someone means embracing differences. You won't always see eye-to-eye, and that's okay. Learn to compromise and find solutions that work for both of you. These are valuable skills that go beyond the college years.

Create a positive atmosphere. Be supportive of each other's goals and aspirations. Celebrate successes and offer a helping hand during challenging times. A positive living environment is essential to a happier college experience.

[17]
PARTICIPATING IN INTRAMURAL SPORTS

Participating in intramural sports during college can be your ticket to fun, fitness, and a fantastic social scene. Let's discuss why getting involved in intramural sports is a game-changer.

To start with, it's all about camaraderie. Intramural sports bring people together like nothing else. Whether you're a seasoned athlete or just trying something new, you'll be part of a community that shares the love for the game.

Fitness meets fun! Say goodbye to monotonous workouts and hello to a dynamic, engaging way to stay fit. Intramural sports offer a range of activities, from traditional team sports like basketball and soccer to more unique options like kickball or ultimate frisbee.

Expand your social circle. College is a melting pot of diverse individuals, and intramural sports are the perfect arenas to meet them. You'll form friendships that go beyond the field or court. Whether you win or lose, the bonds you create through shared victories and challenges will last a lifetime.

Learn life skills. Intramural sports will teach you valuable lessons: teamwork, leadership, communication, and resilience. These skills aren't just for the game; they translate into real-world situations and future endeavors.

[18]
EXPLORING CAMPUS DIVERSITY

College is a melting pot of cultures, backgrounds, and perspectives, and embracing this diversity is a key part of the incredible journey you're on. Let's talk about how you can best explore and celebrate the richness of campus diversity.

One of the more obvious ways you can partake in the diversity of campus is to attend multicultural events. Campuses host a myriad of cultural celebrations, festivals, and awareness weeks. You can also join multicultural clubs and organizations. Colleges usually have a variety of clubs representing different ethnicities, nationalities, and interests.

Engage in open conversations. Be curious and open-minded. Strike up conversations with people from different backgrounds. Share your own experiences and be genuinely interested in theirs.

Take diverse courses. Explore courses that delve into different cultures, histories, and perspectives. This can be a fantastic way to gain academic insight into the diversity around you. Challenge yourself to step outside your comfort zone and broaden your intellectual horizons.

Explore the local community. Venture beyond the campus boundaries and explore the surrounding neighborhoods. Visit cultural establishments, try diverse cuisines, and attend local events.

[19]
UTILIZING HEALTH AND WELLNESS CENTERS

Your college journey isn't just about hitting the books; it's about nurturing your mind and body. One incredible resource at your disposal is the campus health and wellness center, and you'll want to make the most of it. Here's why.

First and foremost, preventive care is essential. The health and wellness center is a convenient, on-campus service that offers vaccinations, screenings, and health education. It's your go-to for staying on top of your health and preventing potential issues before they arise. Regular check-ups are your armor in the battle for well-being.

Health centers give you access to experts who care. They're staffed with healthcare professionals ready to address your concerns. From nurses and doctors to counselors, these experts are there to support you. Got questions about your health or need advice? They've got your back.

Mental health matters! College life can be exhilarating, but also anxiety-inducing. Health and wellness centers often provide counseling services to help you navigate stress, anxiety, or any other mental health concerns you may have. Taking care of your mental well-being is a crucial part of your college success story.

Stay well on a budget. Many services at the health center are either free or available at a reduced cost for students. This is a golden opportunity to prioritize your health without breaking the bank.

[20]
UNDERSTANDING
CAMPUS CULTURE

Stepping into college is like entering a new world, and understanding your campus culture is key to thriving in this vibrant community. Here's your guide to decoding the heartbeat of your college culture.

Observe and absorb. Take the time to contemplate interactions, events, and daily life on campus. Attend orientation activities, explore common areas, and engage with the student body. Pay attention to the unwritten rules and social dynamics that shape the campus culture.

Connect with diverse groups. Your college is a mosaic of people from various backgrounds with unique interests and experiences. Join clubs, organizations, and activities that align with your passions, but also push you out of your comfort zone.

Embrace traditions and rituals. Colleges often have unique traditions and rituals that define their culture. Whether it's a specific event, an annual celebration, or a quirky tradition, participate and immerse yourself in these cultural cornerstones.

Talk to current students and alumni. Both your peers and alumni hold valuable insights into the evolution of campus culture, its nuances, and the events that have shaped it. Their perspectives provide a historical context that deepens your understanding.

Stay informed and involved. Keep up with campus news, announcements, and events. Attend town hall meetings, forums, and campus-wide gatherings.

Be open-minded and adaptable. College cultures evolve, and being flexible is essential. Embrace change, appreciate diversity, and be adaptable. Your willingness to understand and accept different perspectives contributes positively to the evolving tapestry of campus culture.

CHAPTER THREE: FINANCIAL MANAGEMENT

Money management is your ticket to fiscal freedom and learning it early will set you up for success as an adult. Learn to budget, save, and make smart decisions to keep as much money in your pocket as possible. Let's dive into the basics so you can rock your college finances!

[21]
BUDGETING FOR COLLEGE STUDENTS

It might not sound as thrilling as a blockbuster movie, but trust us, budgeting your money in college is the key to unlocking financial independence.

Break down your expenses into categories like tuition, textbooks, housing, food, transportation, and entertainment. This will help you track your money and avoid the dreaded financial kryptonite of debt.

Prioritize your *needs* over your *wants*. Your strength lies in making wise spending decisions. Do you really need that extra-large pizza, or can you settle for a regular one and save some cash? Channel your inner financial warrior and make choices that align with your budget goals.

Next up, the sidekick every college student needs—a part-time job. Whether it's a campus position, internship, or a gig off-campus, having a source of income can rescue you from financial distress. Make sure to balance work with studies so you don't end up overwhelmed.

Another critical budgeting strategy is building an emergency fund. Life is unpredictable, and having a financial safety net can save you when unexpected expenses swoop in.

Finally, beware of credit card traps. While they may seem like easy tools that can help you out of a tricky financial situation, they can quickly lead to a slippery slope of debt. Use them wisely, or you might find yourself facing an uphill financial battle of your own making.

[22]
UNDERSTANDING STUDENT LOANS

Understanding student loans can be a bit overwhelming, particularly if you're handling the process yourself. However, knowing the ins and outs of student loans is crucial for managing your finances.

There are two main types of student loans: federal and private. Federal loans are offered by the government and typically have lower interest rates and more flexible repayment options. Private loans, on the other hand, come from private lenders and may have higher interest rates and stricter terms.

When it comes to federal loans, there are a few different options. Direct Subsidized Loans are based on financial need, and the government pays the interest while you're in school. Direct Unsubsidized Loans are available to all eligible students, but you're responsible for the interest from the beginning. Plus, there are Parent PLUS Loans available for your guardians to help cover educational expenses.

Now, let's talk about repayment. Most federal loans offer a grace period, giving you some time after graduation before you must start making payments. It's crucial to understand your repayment plan options, as there are several, including income-driven repayment plans that base your payments on your income.

Keep an eye on your loan balances, and only borrow what you absolutely need. It's tempting to take out extra funds but remember: You'll have to pay it all back eventually. Be mindful of your budget and prioritize your spending.

If possible, explore scholarships and grants before resorting to loans. Free money is always a win! Finally, keep in mind that there are resources available to help you understand your loan situation better, like your college's financial aid office.

[23]
SCHOLARSHIP AND GRANT OPPORTUNITIES

Now, let's talk about scholarships and grants, which can help you avoid the student loan quagmire. Finding these opportunities might take a bit of effort, but trust us, the payoff is worth it.

Start your search close to home. Check with your school's financial aid office, as they'll have a trove of information on scholarships specific to your college. Your academic advisor can also be a valuable resource, guiding you to opportunities aligned with your field of study.

Next, unleash the power of the internet! Numerous websites like *Fastweb*, *Scholarship.com*, and *College Board* compile thousands of scholarship and grant opportunities. Create profiles, input your details, and let these platforms match you with scholarships tailored to your interests, achievements, and background.

Don't underestimate the impact of local connections. Check with community organizations, foundations, and businesses in your area. They often have scholarships for students from the community for those pursuing specific fields of study.

Keep an eye out for niche scholarships. Whether you're a left-handed artist or a vegetarian environmentalist, there's probably a unique scholarship out there with your name on it. Speaking of uniqueness, find opportunities to showcase your talents and accomplishments. Many scholarships are merit-based, so highlight your achievements in academics, sports, arts, or community service.

Finally, don't forget about government grants. Fill out the Free Application for Federal Student Aid (FAFSA) to be considered for federal grants like the Pell Grant. Explore state and local government programs as well.

[24]
MANAGING CREDIT
CARDS WISELY

As a college student, credit cards can either be your best friend or your worst enemy. Mastering the art of credit card management is crucial during your college years, and we're here to guide you through it.

Before you even *think* about applying for a credit card, get familiar with the basics. Understand terms like APR (Annual Percentage Rate), credit limit, and grace period. APR is the interest rate you'll be charged if you carry a balance, and the credit limit is the maximum amount you can spend. The grace period is the time you have before interest starts accruing on your purchases—pay close attention to this one!

Choose your credit card wisely. Look for cards with no annual fees and low interest rates. Student credit cards are designed with you in mind, often offering perks like cashback rewards. Stick to one or two cards and use them responsibly.

Always pay your bills on time. Late payments not only lead to hefty fees but can also negatively impact your credit score. Set up reminders or automatic payments to ensure you never miss a due date.

Speaking of credit scores, be mindful of your credit utilization ratio—the percentage of your credit limit you're using. Aim to keep your balance below 30% to maintain a healthy credit score.

[25]
SAVING MONEY
ON TEXTBOOKS

After you enroll in college and pay your first tuition bill, you might think your expenses are over for a while—then you get the list of textbooks you'll need. Fortunately, there are savvy ways to save some serious cash on these essentials.

Before you buy a single textbook, be sure to do some comparison shopping. You don't have to purchase your books from the campus bookstore, so check online retailers, rental services, and even consider buying them used. Websites like *Amazon*, *Chegg*, and *BookFinder* can be useful in finding affordable options. Compare prices and go for the best deal—your wallet will thank you.

Consider e-books and digital options. Many textbooks are available in electronic formats, often at a fraction of the cost of their printed counterparts.

In addition, don't overlook the power of borrowing! Check if your school library has the required textbooks available for loan. You might not need them for the entire semester, and borrowing can save you a pretty penny.

Team up with classmates and share the load. Collaborate on textbook purchases or create a rotating system where each person buys one book and you all share. It's a win-win, and you'll all benefit from the collective savings.

Hit the secondhand market—both online and offline. Look for local bookstores, thrift shops, or online marketplaces where students sell or donate their used textbooks. You'll often find well-maintained books at significantly lower prices.

When the semester is over, sell your textbooks and recoup some of your expenses. It's a great way to recycle and recover a portion of your investment and help another student at the same time.

[26]
FINDING PART-TIME JOBS

As we mentioned previously, getting a part-time job while you're in college can help you manage your financial responsibilities. It might feel overwhelming to have a job *and* go to school full time, but it's not as daunting as it sounds.

Visit your college's career center. Not only will they have job boards and other resources for you, but they can help you craft an amazing resume and cover letter.

Networking is the name of the game. Reach out to professors, classmates, and even family friends. Let people know you're on the lookout for a part-time job. Personal connections can open doors you never knew existed.

Explore on-campus opportunities. Colleges often have a variety of positions available for students, from working in the library to assisting with events. These jobs are convenient and usually accommodate the demands of a student's academic schedule, with the added benefit of cutting down on commuting costs.

Consider work-study programs. If you're eligible, federal work-study programs offer on-campus or community service positions for students with financial need. It's a fantastic way to earn money while contributing to the community.

Think local. Check out businesses around your college town—cafes, retail stores, or local services. Many businesses are open to hiring students, and a part-time job nearby can be both convenient and rewarding.

[27]
FINANCIAL AID ESSENTIALS

We've already discussed student loans, scholarships, and grants to some degree, but financial aid may still be something of a mystery to you. Here's some more in-depth information about the essentials you need to know if you're relying on financial aid to fund your college education.

FAFSA (Free Application for Federal Student Aid): This is your golden ticket. Filling out the FAFSA is the first step to unlocking federal grants, loans, and work-study programs. It's the gateway to financial aid, so familiarize yourself with it.

Grants: Think of grants as free money. They're funds you don't have to repay. Federal and state governments, as well as colleges and private organizations, offer grants based on financial need, academic achievement, or other criteria.

Scholarships: Like grants, scholarships are a way to get financial aid without the burden of repayment. They can be merit-based, need-based, or awarded for specific achievements or talents.

Work-Study Programs: These programs provide part-time jobs for students, often related to their field of study or community service. It's a chance to earn money while gaining valuable work experience.

Subsidized and Unsubsidized Loans: Subsidized loans don't accrue interest while you're in school, and the government covers the interest during certain periods. Unsubsidized loans accrue interest from the start, and you're responsible for the interest payments.

[28]
FRUGAL LIVING
TIPS

Even if you're not using loans to fund your college courses, you'll still want to limit your spending—particularly if you're not working a part-time job. Here are some frugal tips to keep your wallet happy without missing out on the college experience.

Cook at Home: Eating out adds up fast. Embrace your inner chef and cook at home. It's not only healthier, but also lighter on your wallet. Plan ahead, buy in bulk, and watch your savings grow.

Take Advantage of Student Discounts: Your student ID is more than just a ticket to the library. Many places offer student discounts—from restaurants to entertainment venues. Flash that ID and enjoy the perks.

Embrace Thrifting: Thrift stores are treasure troves for those on a budget. Whether you're looking for clothes, furniture, or unique finds, thrift shopping is budget-friendly and eco-conscious. It's a win-win!

Limit Impulse Buys: Before hitting the checkout, ask yourself if it's a need or a want. Impulse buys can derail your budget quickly. Give yourself a cool-off period before making non-essential purchases.

Use Public Transportation: Cars can be costly. If possible, use public transportation or opt for a bike. It's not only economical, but also environmentally friendly.

Attend Free Events: Colleges often host free events, from guest lectures to cultural performances. Take advantage of these opportunities without spending a dime.

[29]
PLANNING FOR
FUTURE EXPENSES

Planning for future expenses on a tight budget might feel like navigating uncharted waters. However, with a bit of strategic thinking, you can set yourself up for financial success down the road.

The best tip we can provide is to build an emergency fund. Even if it's just a small portion of your income each month, having a safety net can be a game-changer for unexpected expenses, like medical bills or sudden equipment breakdowns.

Prioritize the essentials, including rent, utilities, and groceries. Ensure these non-negotiable expenses are covered first before allocating money to other categories.

Set clear financial goals. Whether it's saving for a trip, paying off student loans, or building long-term wealth, having specific goals gives your financial planning purpose. Break them down into achievable steps.

Craft a realistic budget that reflects your current income. Be honest about what you can afford and allocate funds for both needs and wants.

Review this budget regularly; as your circumstances change, so should your financial plan.

Explore side hustles or part-time gigs if your schedule allows. Whether it's freelancing, tutoring, or a campus job, a little extra income can go a long way.

Stay informed about potential financial aid opportunities, grants, and scholarships. Keep an eye on eligibility criteria and application deadlines. Every bit of aid can alleviate the financial burden.

By planning wisely, setting realistic goals, and making informed choices, you lay the foundation for a financially empowered journey beyond college.

[30]
AVOIDING
FINANCIAL SCAMS

Before we end this section on financial management, we need to talk about a real-world challenge that can sneak up on anyone: financial scams. As you navigate the exciting world of college, it's crucial to stay vigilant and protect your hard-earned money from those looking to take advantage.

Be wary of unsolicited emails and messages. If it sounds too good to be true, it probably is. Scammers often use phishing emails or fake messages to trick you into revealing personal information or clicking on malicious links. Never share sensitive details online, such as your Social Security Number or bank information, unless it's absolutely necessary and with a trusted institution.

Use secure Wi-Fi networks. Avoid accessing sensitive information on public Wi-Fi networks, as they may not be secure. If you need to use public Wi-Fi, consider using a virtual private network (VPN) for added security.

Watch out for fake job offers. Scammers sometimes pose as employers, offering too-good-to-be-true jobs or internships. Research the company, verify the job offer, and be cautious if someone asks for payment or personal information upfront.

Be skeptical of requests for—or offers of—money. Whether it's a new online friend or a supposed emergency involving a family member, think twice before you do anything. Scammers use emotional stories to exploit your kindness, so always verify the legitimacy of such requests.

Keep an eye on your financial accounts. Regularly review your bank and credit card statements for any unauthorized transactions and report any suspicious activity to your bank or credit card company immediately.

CHAPTER FOUR:
PERSONAL
DEVELOPMENT

[31]
DEVELOPING
SOFT SKILLS

As you make your way through college, it's important to recognize that success in the professional world goes beyond mastering textbooks and acing exams. Developing "soft skills" is a fundamental aspect of your college experience that will significantly impact your future endeavors.

Soft skills are skills developed to help you work harmoniously with others and navigate the challenges of life. While your academic achievements showcase your knowledge and expertise, it's your soft skills that will set you apart in the competitive landscape of the professional world.

One essential soft skill is effective communication, which is the ability to articulate your thoughts clearly, listen actively, and express ideas in a succinct manner. Whether you're collaborating on group projects or participating in discussions, honing your communication skills will enhance your overall academic and professional performance.

Adaptability is another crucial soft skill to learn. The world is constantly evolving, and the ability to embrace change, learn from new experiences, and adjust your approach accordingly is vital.

Collaboration and teamwork are integral aspects of many professions. Cultivating the ability to work effectively with diverse groups of people, understand different perspectives, and contribute positively to team dynamics will serve you well in college and beyond.

In addition, time management, critical thinking, and problem-solving are soft skills that can greatly enhance your college experience and future success. Invest time and effort in developing these soft skills; they're the key to unlocking a future full of possibilities.

[32]
STRESS MANAGEMENT STRATEGIES

College life can be exhilarating, but it often comes with its fair share of challenges and stressors. Balancing academics, social life, and personal responsibilities can sometimes feel overwhelming. Because of this, adopting effective stress-management strategies is crucial for your well-being and success.

Prioritize and Plan

Take a proactive approach to your responsibilities by creating a realistic schedule. Prioritize tasks based on deadlines and importance. Breaking down larger tasks into smaller, more manageable steps can make them less daunting.

Practice Self-Care

It's easy to neglect self-care during busy times, but taking care of your physical and mental well-being is paramount. Ensure you get enough sleep, eat nourishing meals, and make time for relaxing activities that recharge your mental batteries.

Stay Active

Regular physical activity has been shown to reduce stress and boost your mood. Find an exercise routine that suits your preferences, whether it's hitting the gym, going for a run, participating in a group sport, or practicing yoga.

Mindfulness and Relaxation Techniques

Incorporate mindfulness practices such as deep breathing, meditation, or progressive muscle relaxation into your routine. These techniques can help calm your mind and alleviate stress.

Seek Help When Needed

If stress becomes overwhelming, don't hesitate to seek help from campus counseling services or other mental health professionals. It's a sign of strength to recognize when you need support.

[33]
BUILDING
SELF-CONFIDENCE

As you probably know, building and maintaining confidence is an ongoing process. However, with dedication and self-reflection, you can cultivate a strong sense of self-esteem. Here are some strategies to boost your confidence during your college years.

Acknowledge Your Achievements

Take time to recognize and celebrate your accomplishments, both big and small. Whether it's acing a test, completing a challenging assignment, or overcoming a personal obstacle, acknowledging your achievements will reinforce your capabilities.

Embrace Failure as a Learning Opportunity

Understand that setbacks and failures are integral parts of any journey. Instead of viewing them as obstacles, see them as opportunities for growth. Analyze what went wrong, learn from the experience, and use that knowledge to improve.

Step Outside Your Comfort Zone

Growth occurs when you challenge yourself. Embrace new experiences, whether it's joining a club, participating in public speaking, or trying out for a team. Stepping outside your comfort zone will build your resilience and confidence.

Positive Self-Talk

Monitor your inner dialogue and replace self-doubt with positive affirmations. Remind yourself of your strengths, capabilities, and past successes.

Develop Skills and Expertise

Invest time in developing your skills and knowledge in areas of interest. Becoming proficient in a particular subject or mastering a skill not only enhances your competence, but also boosts your confidence in your abilities.

Surround Yourself with Supportive People

Build a network of positive and supportive individuals who uplift and encourage you. Surrounding yourself with people who believe in your potential can have a profound impact on your confidence.

[34]
TIME FOR
SELF-REFLECTION

No matter what stage of life you're in, it's essential to carve out moments for self-reflection, and this is especially true for college students. Amid the whirlwind of academic pressures, social engagements, and responsibilities, the act of introspection might appear to be a luxury, but its significance cannot be overstated.

Self-reflection is a journey into the core of your values and beliefs. In understanding what truly matters to you, you forge an alliance between your choices and your authentic self, fostering a sense of purpose and fulfillment.

Practicing self-reflection also contributes to emotional intelligence, allowing you to understand and manage your emotions effectively. This skill is pivotal for building meaningful relationships and succeeding in various life situations.

When faced with challenges, self-reflection enhances your problem-solving skills. It encourages a thoughtful approach, helping you explore different perspectives and strategies for resolution.

Ultimately, self-reflection is a catalyst for personal growth. It empowers you to consciously evolve, refining your character, skills, and outlook on life. During the controlled chaos of college life, think of self-reflection not merely as a pause, but as an investment in your personal growth.

[35]
SETTING PERSONAL GOALS

College is an exciting chapter of your life, filled with possibilities, and setting personal goals gives you a compass to guide you through this adventure. Goals provide direction, purpose, and a roadmap for personal growth. Here's why setting personal goals is essential during your college experience.

Clarity of Purpose

Personal goals help you define your purpose in college, because they provide a sense of direction and intent to your journey.

Motivation and Focus

Goals serve as powerful motivators. They give you a reason to strive for excellence and focus your efforts on what truly matters to you. When you're faced with challenges, your goals serve as the driving force that propels you forward.

Measurable Progress

Breaking down larger goals into smaller, more measurable steps will allow you to track your progress. Celebrating these incremental victories will not only boost your confidence, but keep you motivated to reach the next milestone, as well.

Time Management

College life can be demanding; you're forced to juggle classes, assignments, and social activities on your own. Setting realistic timelines for your goals fosters effective time management skills.

Balancing Academic and Personal Life

Personal goals extend beyond academics, including aspects of personal well-being, relationships, and hobbies. Setting goals in these areas promotes a balanced and fulfilling college experience.

Adaptability and Growth

College is a time of exploration and self-discovery. Your goals should be adaptable to allow for growth and change. Your life will be filled with change, and your goals should reflect these changes.

[36]
OVERCOMING PROCRASTINATION

Procrastination, the perpetual nemesis of productivity, is a common obstacle many students face during their college journey. It's time to confront this challenge head-on through a combination of self-awareness, effective strategies, and a commitment to your goals.

To begin with, it's necessary to understand the root cause of your procrastination. Is it fear of failure, lack of motivation, feeling overwhelmed, or something deeper? Identifying the underlying issues is an important step towards finding targeted solutions.

Break down each task into smaller, more manageable chunks. The sheer magnitude of some projects can be intimidating, leading to procrastination. By dividing a project into bite-sized steps, you make the workload more digestible and less overwhelming by setting realistic goals.

Establish a routine that incorporates both work and leisure. Consistency is key, and sticking to a structured schedule creates a conducive environment for productivity.

Ensure your study area is organized, free from distractions, and tailored to your preferences. A well-arranged space, used only for schoolwork, can enhance focus and minimize procrastination.

Reward yourself for completing tasks. Positive reinforcement encourages the habit of timely accomplishment. Celebrate your victories, no matter how small, to cultivate a positive association with productivity.

[37]
NURTURING CREATIVITY

Your college years are when the pursuit of knowledge mingles with a blossoming of imaginative thinking. Creativity is not just for the arts — it's a life skill that will serve you well across any field or profession.

To begin the process, embrace curiosity like an old friend. The desire to understand, explore, and question serves as creative fuel. Don't be afraid to venture into the unknown, for uncertainty is often where the seeds of innovation lie. Let your inquisitive nature be the compass that guides you through the labyrinth of inspiration.

Remember, creativity thrives in diversity. Surround yourself with people from different backgrounds and disciplines with unique perspectives. Engage in conversations that challenge your beliefs and be open to seeing the world through someone else's lens. It's in this mosaic of ideas that your creativity will find its most vibrant colors.

Failure is not the end of the road; each stumble is an opportunity to learn, adapt, and evolve. Don't fear mistakes, but rather, embrace them as part of the creative process. Allow your slip-ups to shape your resilience and fortify your determination.

Develop habits that cultivate creativity. Dedicate time to activities that inspire you, whether reading, taking walks, or indulging in hobbies. These moments of respite often result in the most profound breakthroughs.

Finally, learn to be patient with yourself. Creativity is not a sprint — it's a marathon. You'll experience moments of stagnation, but these are essential for the next surge of inspiration. Trust the process, and in due time, your ideas will unfurl like a tapestry of transformation.

[38]
MAINTAINING PHYSICAL HEALTH

As you take on academic challenges and experience the newfound independence of college life, it's crucial not to overlook the importance of maintaining your physical health. The infamous "freshman 15" is a real concern, but with some mindful choices and a commitment to regular physical activity, you can steer clear of this common pitfall.

Pay attention to your eating habits. The dining hall may offer an array of tempting options but try to strike a balance between indulgence and nutrition. Incorporate fruits, vegetables, lean proteins, and whole grains into your meals. Don't skip breakfast and stay hydrated by drinking plenty of water throughout the day. Consider smaller, more frequent meals to keep your metabolism in motion.

Scheduling regular exercise is also vital for your overall well-being. Find an activity you enjoy, whether it's hitting the gym, joining a sports club, or taking fitness classes. Physical activity not only helps you maintain a healthy weight, but also boosts your mood, reduces stress, and improves concentration.

Don't underestimate the power of incorporating movement into your daily routine. Walk or bike instead of driving or taking the bus, use stairs instead of elevators, and take short breaks during study sessions to stretch or go for a quick walk. Small lifestyle changes can make a significant impact on your physical health.

Finally, aim for 7-9 hours of sleep each night to support your overall health. College life can be demanding, but ensuring you get enough rest is paramount for both physical and mental health.

[39]
EMOTIONAL
INTELLIGENCE

Have you ever heard of emotional intelligence? College life isn't just about acing exams; it's all about understanding and managing your own emotions and being tuned into what others are feeling. College is a crash course in life, and it's the perfect time to boost your emotional intelligence (or EI).

First off, the social scene in college is diverse. Joining clubs, working on group projects, and getting involved in activities that force you to interact with all types of people will all help develop your EI.

It's no surprise that college is full of challenges. You'll face stress, maybe fail a test or two, and deal with disappointments. However, these are golden opportunities to figure out how to bounce back and handle your emotions. Learning to cope with setbacks and stress is important for developing emotional resilience.

Don't forget your professors and advisors! They're not just there to give you grades — they can serve as part of your emotional support squad. Share your feelings, ask for feedback, and gain insight from their experience.

If you're looking for more ways to expand your EI, try diving into extracurriculars. Volunteering, internships, and community service throw you into situations where you need killer communication and teamwork skills, as well as an understanding of different viewpoints.

Essentially, college is your EI training ground. Embrace the social whirlwind, tackle the ups and downs of academics, develop relationships with mentors, and dive into new activities. You'll come out the other side with top-notch emotional intelligence that'll set you up for success in life, not just school.

[40]
CULTIVATE
RESILIENCE

As you've no doubt learned, the college years are an exciting and challenging time in your life. As you tackle academic and personal challenges, cultivating resilience is a crucial skill that will empower you to overcome obstacles and thrive in the face of adversity.

Before you can develop resilience, you must acknowledge that setbacks and failures are a natural part of the learning process. Rather than viewing them as insurmountable obstacles, see them as valuable lessons that contribute to your overall development.

Building a support network is essential. Surround yourself with positive and like-minded individuals who can provide encouragement during tough times. Sharing your struggles with others not only lightens the burden but also allows you to benefit from different points of view.

Effective time management is another key aspect of resilience. As we've mentioned, it can be helpful to break down large tasks into more manageable steps. Establishing a routine and setting realistic goals will also help you stay organized and focused.

Learn to adapt to change and uncertainty. College life is dynamic, and unexpected challenges may arise. Developing flexibility and a willingness to adjust your plans will help you navigate these uncertainties with greater ease. Embrace opportunities to develop problem-solving skills and find creative solutions.

Self-care is often underestimated, but it's crucial for building resilience. Maintaining your physical and mental well-being allows you to approach challenges with a clear mind and a stronger sense of resilience.

Keep in mind that resilience is not about avoiding difficulties; it allows you to bounce back stronger and more capable than before. Embrace challenges as opportunities for growth on your journey through college and beyond.

CHAPTER FIVE: CAREER PLANNING

College is a pivotal time to shape your future. Effective career planning involves more than just choosing a major—it includes aligning your passions, skills, and goals. In this section, we'll explore strategic steps to help you set a strong foundation for your future career.

[41]
RESUME AND COVER LETTER WRITING

The path to your dream job begins with a masterful resume and cover letter. These documents are personal marketing tools; they'll make you stand out in a sea of applicants.

Start with a Strong Foundation

Your resume should begin with your contact information, followed by a clear and concise objective or summary statement. Highlight your career goals and what makes you unique but keep it short and sweet—employers appreciate brevity.

Showcase Your Education

For college students, education is often the most relevant section. List your university, major, graduation date, and any honors or relevant coursework. If you have a high GPA, include it as well.

Highlight Experience and Skills

Next, detail your work experience and skills. Focus on internships, part-time jobs, or volunteer work related to your field of study. Use bullet points to describe your responsibilities and achievements. Showcase your transferable skills, such as communication, teamwork, and problem-solving.

Tailor Your Resume

Customize your resume for each application. Analyze the job description and emphasize skills and experiences that align with the position. This shows employers that you've done your homework and are genuinely interested.

Craft a Standout Cover Letter

Your cover letter is your chance to tell your story. Start with a strong opening that grabs attention. Briefly explain why you're interested in the position and how your skills align with the company's needs. Share a specific accomplishment or experience that demonstrates your qualifications. If possible, include the name of the hiring manager who will receive your application.

Be Professional and Proofread

Keep your resume and cover letter professional in tone and appearance. Check for grammatical errors and typos—attention to detail matters!

[42]
INTERNSHIP SEARCH STRATEGIES

The internship hunt can be both exciting and overwhelming, but with the right strategies, you can successfully navigate this journey.

First and foremost, start early! Don't wait until the last minute to kick off your search. Many companies recruit interns months in advance, so begin exploring opportunities well before your desired internship period. This proactive approach increases your chance of finding a position that aligns with your goals.

Networking is another crucial aspect. Attend career fairs, industry events, and connect with professionals on *LinkedIn*. Building a robust network can provide insights into potential opportunities and expose you to different career paths.

Use your resume and cover letter to highlight relevant skills, experiences, and achievements. Your application forms your first impression, so make it stand out. Research the company thoroughly and demonstrate how your skills align with their needs.

Take advantage of your university's career services. They offer resources like resume reviews, mock interviews, and job search workshops. Use these services to fine-tune your application and enhance your interview skills.

Explore company websites, industry-specific platforms, and professional organizations related to your field to find less-obvious opportunities. Be persistent — rejections are part of the process. Learn from each experience, seek feedback, and keep refining your approach.

[43]
NETWORKING FUNDAMENTALS

When you start your job search, you'll realize how important it is to build a network that extends beyond the classroom. Networking involves cultivating meaningful connections with professionals in your field of interest. Here are some fundamental principles to guide you in forming a robust professional network that can help you land your dream job.

First and foremost, authenticity is key. Be genuine in your interactions with others, expressing your true self and interests. Authenticity fosters trust and establishes a solid foundation for lasting professional relationships. Whether you're attending networking events, joining professional organizations, or engaging on social media, remember to be true to yourself.

Effective communication is another vital aspect of networking. Hone your ability to articulate your goals, experiences, and strengths succinctly. Practice your "elevator pitch" — a compelling, 30-second summary of who you are and what you're seeking professionally.

Reciprocity is a principle that should guide your networking efforts. Offer your support and expertise to others in your network, creating a mutually beneficial environment in which everyone can thrive.

Building and maintaining relationships require consistency. Stay connected with your network through regular calls, emails, or meetups.

Don't forget to embrace diversity in your network. Connect with professionals from various backgrounds, industries, and experiences. A diverse network exposes you to different perspectives, opening doors to unforeseen opportunities and enriching your overall professional development.

[44]
ATTENDING
CAREER FAIRS

During your college experience, you'll undoubtedly attend career fairs. These fairs can be both exciting and a bit overwhelming, but if you prepare yourself before you attend, you can make the most of these valuable opportunities.

Do Your Research

Research the companies that will be attending the career fair. Knowing their values, goals, and recent projects not only showcases your genuine interest, but also helps you tailor your conversations with recruiters.

Dress to Impress

It's cliché but true—first impressions matter. Choose professional attire that aligns with the industry you're interested in. Whether it's a suit and tie or business casual, dressing well reflects your respect for the potential employers you'll be engaging with.

Pass Out That Resume

Bring multiple copies of your resume. You never know how many recruiters you'll meet, and having extra copies shows you're prepared and serious about exploring opportunities.

Practice your elevator pitch

This concise introduction should convey who you are, your major, and what you're looking for in a career. Keep it short and engaging and rehearse it until it feels natural. Confidence goes a long way toward making a lasting impression.

Follow Up

Collect business cards or contact information from recruiters and express your gratitude for their time. Mention specific details from your conversation to jog their memory and reiterate your interest in their company.

[45]
PREPARING FOR
JOB INTERVIEWS

When you start to land job interviews, you'll discover that attending career fairs and meeting with recruiters is very similar to the interview process. Most of the tips that lead to success at career fairs will also serve you well in interviews.

Research, Research, Research: Before you step into the interview room, know the company inside and out. Understand its values, culture, and recent achievements. This knowledge will not only impress your interviewer but will also help you tailor your responses to align with the company's goals.

Polish Your Resume: Your resume is your personal marketing tool. Ensure it's updated, error-free, and that it highlights your key achievements and skills. Be ready to discuss anything mentioned on your resume in detail.

Practice Answering Questions: Anticipate common interview questions and practice your responses. This will boost your confidence and ensure you convey your thoughts clearly. Questions like "Tell me about yourself" and "What are your strengths and weaknesses?" are classics.

Dress the Part: Remember, first impressions matter. Dress professionally and ensure your outfit conforms to the company's dress code. It's always better to be slightly overdressed than underdressed.

Showcase Your Soft Skills: While technical skills are important, employers also value soft skills like communication, teamwork, and adaptability. Be prepared to share examples of how you've demonstrated these skills in the past.

Ask Thoughtful Questions: Impress your interviewer by preparing thoughtful questions about the company, team dynamics, and the role itself. This demonstrates your genuine interest in the position.

Follow Up: Send a thank-you email within 24 hours of the interview expressing your gratitude for the opportunity. It's a simple gesture that reinforces your interest in working for their company.

[46]
UNDERSTANDING
WORKPLACE ETIQUETTE

Once you leave college and venture into the professional world, understanding workplace etiquette will be crucial for a successful transition from academia to the workforce. Here are some essential tips to help you navigate the nuances of the professional environment.

Punctuality Matters

Being on time is a simple yet significant aspect of workplace etiquette. Arriving punctually for meetings and completing assignments on time reflects your commitment to the job.

Dress Professionally

Dress codes vary across industries, but it's essential to present yourself professionally. Pay attention to the company culture, and dress accordingly. Appropriate attire contributes to a positive first impression and demonstrates your seriousness about your role.

Effective Communication

Clear and concise communication is key in the workplace. Practice active listening, articulate your thoughts, and be open to feedback. Professionalism extends beyond verbal communication to include emails, where maintaining a respectful and formal tone is crucial.

Respect Diversity

Today's workplaces are diverse, and respecting different perspectives is vital. Be inclusive, avoid making assumptions, and embrace the richness that diversity brings to the team.

Mind Your Digital Presence

Social media is a powerful tool, but it can also impact your professional reputation. Be mindful of what you share online, especially when it comes to work-related matters.

Learn the Office Culture

Each workplace has its own unique culture. Observe how things are done, ask questions, and adapt accordingly. Understanding and embracing the company culture will help you integrate seamlessly into the team.

Teamwork and Collaboration

Collaboration is a cornerstone of many workplaces. Be a team player by offering help when needed, sharing credit, and respecting your colleagues' contributions.

[47]
EXPLORING
CAREER PATHS

The incredible number of potential career paths you'll be exposed to in college can be mind-boggling. Luckily, there are ways to explore your options without committing to a full-time job right away.

As we mentioned, internships can provide a taste of the real-world work environment without the commitment of a permanent job. Seek opportunities in various fields to get hands-on experience and determine if the day-to-day tasks align with your expectations. Many companies offer internships during the summer or part-time during the school year.

Networking is another powerful tool. Join relevant clubs, organizations, or online communities related to your interests. This not only enhances your knowledge, but also exposes you to potential mentors. You might be surprised how many doors will open through a simple conversation!

Don't underestimate the value of informational interviews. Reach out to professionals in your desired field and request a casual chat. Learn about their career paths, challenges, and successes. It's an excellent way to gain insight and expand your network.

Volunteer work is another avenue for exploration. Non-profit organizations and community projects often welcome enthusiastic volunteers.

[48]
BUILDING AN
ONLINE PRESENCE

In today's digital age, establishing a solid online presence is crucial, both personally and professionally. Whether you're gearing up for internships, job searches, or just want to connect with like-minded individuals, here are some "dos" and "don'ts" to help you navigate the virtual world.

Dos:

Professional Profile Picture: Use a clear and professional-looking profile picture. It doesn't have to be a headshot from a fancy photoshoot but avoid using overly casual or party photos.

Create a LinkedIn Profile: *LinkedIn* is a goldmine for networking and job opportunities. Craft a comprehensive profile with your education, skills, and experiences. Connect with classmates, professors, and professionals in your field.

Showcase Your Achievements: Don't be shy about highlighting your accomplishments. Share your academic achievements, projects, and any relevant extracurricular activities.

Regularly Update Your Profiles: Keep your online presence current. Update your profiles with new skills, experiences, and achievements. An active and evolving online persona demonstrates your commitment to personal and professional growth.

Don'ts:

Overly Personal Information: While it's great to showcase your personality, avoid oversharing personal information. Maintain a balance between authenticity and professionalism.

Negative or Controversial Content: Think twice before posting negative comments or controversial content. Your online presence reflects your character, and potential employers may scrutinize your digital footprint.

Ignore Privacy Settings: Adjust your privacy settings to control who can see your content. This is especially important if you want to keep your personal and professional life separate.

Neglect Online Etiquette: Be mindful of your tone and language online. Respond to messages and comments politely and avoid engaging in online arguments.

[49]
LONG-TERM
CAREER PLANNING

College is a pivotal time in your life, and while your immediate focus should be on classes, exams, and social experiences, it's crucial to consider your future, too. Long-term career planning may seem daunting, but taking small steps now can set the stage for a fulfilling professional future.

First, explore your interests and passions. What excites you? What subjects or activities make time fly by? Identify your strengths and weaknesses to get a clear picture of where your skills lie.

Again, networking is a key element in long-term career planning. Build relationships with professors, classmates, and professionals in your field of interest. Attend career fairs, workshops, and in-person networking events to connect with industry experts.

Internships and part-time jobs are instrumental to gaining practical experience and understanding your chosen field. Seek opportunities related to your major or career interests, as hands-on experience is often more valuable than theoretical knowledge.

As you progress, create a realistic timeline for your career goals. As with all goals, you should break them down into their smallest components. This can include completing specific courses, gaining relevant certifications, or securing internships between semesters.

Lastly, stay adaptable. Career paths are rarely linear, and unexpected opportunities or challenges may arise. Be open to exploring new possibilities and adjust your plans accordingly. Long-term career planning is about creating a roadmap, but it's okay to take detours as you grow.

[50]
ALUMNI
NETWORKING

We've already discussed how important it is to develop a professional network, but don't overlook the value of alumni networking. This involves connecting with individuals who've walked the same path you're on, providing access to invaluable resources to guide you toward fulfilling careers.

Alumni networking is not a mere exchange of business cards or LinkedIn connections; it's establishing meaningful relationships with those who've successfully transitioned to the professional realm. These connections provide insights into various industries, careers, and real-world applications of your academic pursuits.

Engaging with alumni from your college offers you a unique perspective on practical aspects of your chosen field. Attending alumni events, seminars, or career fairs gains you access to a wealth of knowledge and advice, as well as potential mentorships.

Furthermore, alumni often serve as bridges to job opportunities. Many employers prioritize hiring candidates with connections to their alma mater, recognizing shared values and educational foundation. By participating in alumni networking events, you increase your visibility within professional circles, potentially opening doors to internships, job offers, or informational interviews.

Alumni networking is a powerful tool for college students seeking to develop successful careers. Leverage these connections to gain insights, advice, and even job opportunities.

CHAPTER SIX:
LIFE SKILLS

As you embark on your college experience, mastering life skills is the secret ingredient for success. From time management to budgeting, these tools will serve you well in navigating the campus jungle.

[51]
COOKING
BASIC MEALS

Between classes, assignments, and the constant hustle, cooking might be the last thing on your mind. However, knowing how to whip up basic meals in your dorm room or apartment can be a game-changer for your budget, health, and taste buds. Let's dive into the culinary adventure — no kitchen required!

Before you cook anything, invest in some key tools: a microwave-safe bowl, a cutting board, a knife, and an electric kettle. These simple items will provide your living space with a makeshift kitchen.

Start your day with a power-packed breakfast. Grab instant oats, add hot water from your electric kettle, and customize with fruits, nuts, or a dollop of peanut butter for a tasty kick. It's quick, easy, and keeps you fueled for those early-morning lectures.

Lunch can be a breeze with no-cook options like wraps or sandwiches loaded with veggies, deli meats, and your favorite spreads. Toss in some pre-cut veggies on the side for a crunchy twist. Don't forget to keep your fridge stocked with essentials like yogurt, cheese, and fresh produce.

Dinner is where the microwave takes center stage. Try microwavable rice pouches and veggies for a quick stir-fry. Spice it up with soy sauce or your favorite spices. Canned tuna or chicken can be your go-to protein boost. Experiment with seasonings to elevate flavors!

[52]
DOING LAUNDRY
EFFICIENTLY

Laundry isn't the most thrilling part of campus life, but it's a necessary evil. First up, sort your laundry like a pro. Trust us — separating those whites, darks, and colors will save you from any unexpected tie-dye disasters. It's the oldest trick in the book for a reason.

Washing machines can be intimidating, especially if you've never used one before. Select the right temperature for your clothes — cold for colors, warm for regular stuff, and hot for those seriously-stained pieces. When it comes to detergent, less is more; you don't need to drown your clothes in suds.

When the washing cycle is done, remove your wet clothes promptly to avoid that mildew smell that comes with leaving them in the machine too long. Put clothes that are dryer-friendly into the dryer and set the proper temperature to avoid shrinkage. Anything that can't be dried in the dryer should be hung up or spread on a flat surface and allowed to air dry. Check the label if you're not sure.

While your clothes are in the wash, use that time wisely. Knock out some studying, catch up on assignments, or even hit the gym. Efficiency is the name of the game! When the dryer buzzer goes off, don't let those clothes turn into a wrinkled mess. Empty the machine promptly, and if you're not a fan of folding (who is?), invest in some space-savvy hangers.

[53]
BASIC
FIRST AID

One aspect of college life that you might not have considered is that you're on your own if you get hurt, at least until you can find help. Life on campus can get hectic, and being prepared for unexpected situations can make a world of difference.

Cuts and Scrapes

Keep a first aid kit in your dorm. When you get a minor cut or scrape, clean it with mild soap and water. Apply an antiseptic ointment, then cover it with a sterile bandage. Regularly change the dressing to avoid infection.

Burns

Whether it's a cooking mishap or a curling-iron incident, burns can happen. Run cool (not cold) water over the burn for at least 10 minutes. Avoid using ice. Cover it with a clean, non-stick bandage to protect the skin.

Sprains and Strains

Campus life often involves physical activities. If you twist an ankle or strain a muscle, remember R.I.C.E. — Rest, Ice, Compression, and Elevation. Give your body time to heal, ice the affected area, use a compression bandage, and elevate the injured limb.

Allergic Reactions

Food allergies and insect bites are common triggers of allergic reactions. If you have difficulty breathing, swelling, or a rash, seek immediate medical help. Always carry any prescribed allergy medication, like an epinephrine auto-injector.

Fever and Flu

College campuses are breeding grounds for germs. Rest, stay hydrated, and stock over-the-counter medications for fever or pain relief. If symptoms persist, consult campus health services.

Nosebleed

Pinch your nostrils together and lean forward slightly. Avoid tilting your head backward, as it may cause blood to flow into your throat. Apply pressure for about 10 minutes until the bleeding stops.

[54]
PERSONAL SAFETY
TIPS

Earlier, we discussed campus safety, covering tactics such as using the buddy system, keeping your belongings locked up, and trusting your gut. Those practices are important, but there are others that are necessary for navigating the off-campus world.

Keep Your Drink Covered

When out with your friends, it is important to always watch your drink. It doesn't matter what gender you are, what you order, or how many people you're with; do *not* leave your drink unattended. There are many products, such as drink covers, that are designed to lower the chances of someone drugging your beverage. Otherwise, get in the habit of always covering the top of your glass with your hand. It's also a good idea to stay informed about what common drugs look and taste like, which bars and restaurants have had issues in the past, and what to do if you don't feel well after a drink.

Keep Informed and Alert

Unfortunately, sex trafficking has become more common, especially around campuses. The tactics change with the times, so it is a good idea to stay informed about the most recent tips and warnings specific to your area. For example, at the time this book was written, one common tactic was to apply chloroform to a paper towel and leave it somewhere on the victim's vehicle. When the person removes the towel, they pass out and can be taken. Pay attention to anything out of place or different about your surroundings, and don't touch any foreign objects with your bare hands.

Vary Your Travel Routine

Sometimes, it's impossible to know if someone is watching you. While you don't want to be paranoid, it's a good idea to avoid taking the same routes at the same time every day. When possible, travel with buddies.

Pay attention to your surroundings, and if you think you're being followed, make your way to a police station or hospital.

Share Your Location

Smart phones can track and share your location, and you should take advantage of this feature. Share your location with two or three people you trust. At least one of these people should be someone that checks it frequently, usually an older relative that you trust. You should also share your location with a good friend who lives close by and can help find you if something seems wrong.

Take Caution When Dating

Before accepting a date, make sure to create a safety plan and update your support network about your whereabouts. With online dating becoming increasingly popular, it is especially important to remember that you don't know these people yet. For first dates, choose a public place you know well, somewhere the bartender or hostess knows you and your friends, so they can help keep an eye out for you. If possible, go on a double date with a friend, or have your friends take a table in the same restaurant or bar. If these options aren't feasible, discreetly take a photo of your date's license plate and send it to the people you've shared your location with. Tell them the name of the person you're going out with, too.

Create a Plan A and B and C

Keep a list of phone numbers that are readily available to call in an emergency. One of these people should be a night owl that stays up late, and at least one should have a more relaxed schedule than you and your peers. You don't want to have an emergency at 2 a.m. and get sent straight to voicemail! If all your emergency contacts have classes and a part-time job, you might not be able to get ahold of them when it's most needed. Whoever you ask to help you with this, make sure to offer to do it for them in return, and let them know what times you're available to help.

[55]
PUBLIC TRANSPORTATION
AND NAVIGATION

Navigating public transportation can be a game-changer, especially if you don't have a personal vehicle. Here's a guide to help you master the art of using public transportation.

Get a Transit Map

Start by grabbing a transit map for your city. Most public transportation systems have detailed maps that show routes, stops, and connections. Familiarize yourself with the routes you'll be using frequently.

Purchase a Transit Pass

Look into monthly or semester-based passes; they can save you money compared to individual tickets. Make sure to have your student ID handy to get a discount.

Plan Your Routes

Use online trip planners or mobile apps to map out your routes in advance. Build enough time into your schedule to account for potential delays or unexpected changes, including any transfer points.

Learn the Basics

Understand the different types of public transportation available, including buses, trains, trams, and subways. Each mode has specific rules and etiquette, so make sure you're aware of them.

Stay Connected

Keep your smartphone charged, and download transit apps for real-time updates on schedules and service disruptions. This can be a lifesaver when you're on the go and need to adjust your plans.

Explore Walking and Biking Options

For short distances, consider walking or biking. It's not only healthy but also a great way to explore your campus and local area.

[56]
DAILY LIFE
MANAGEMENT

Here are some practical tips to help you seamlessly integrate effective time management into your daily routine, fostering academic excellence and personal well-being.

Habits and Routines

Creating habits and routines that cover the basic daily building blocks for a healthy life goes a long way. Every day, you need to eat, exercise, get dressed, take care of hygiene, organize your space and belongings for the day, and complete certain tasks toward your goal. Making these tasks daily habit removes the need to think or stress about your schedule. Create a morning and evening routine that bookend your day, and no matter how busy you get, be sure to stick to these routines. The more consistent you are, the less brainpower you'll need to follow through.

Prioritize

It's important to have a clear idea of what's most important to you and what your body and mind need to stay healthy. Social time might be a high priority, especially when you're stressed, as it can help ground you and prevent burnout. Maintain an accurate and objective understanding of what's actually a priority and what can be put on hold. Keep in mind, your priorities don't remain static—sometimes a certain class will need more attention than another. Learning to analyze your tasks and separate what you want from what you need will help tremendously. Keep in mind that your mental health is sometimes more important than extracurricular activities or perfect scores.

Leave Pockets of Open Time

If you plan every second of your day, you increase the chance of burnout. When building a schedule, leave time for spontaneity. You might not always want to use that time to socialize, but it gives you space to do whatever you want—whether it's getting ahead on an assignment or binge-watching a Netflix show.

Avoid Multi-Tasking

While juggling multiple activities might seem like an efficient strategy, it often leads to subpar results. Instead, fully immerse yourself in one activity before moving onto the next. Give yourself a set amount of time for each activity, set timers, eliminate distractions, and give your full attention to the task at hand.

Say "No"

Learn to say "no" when necessary. College life is full of exciting opportunities, but overcommitting can quickly lead to exhaustion. Prioritize your academic commitments, and engage in extracurricular activities selectively, ensuring a healthy balance between your studies and personal life.

[57]
EFFECTIVE COMMUNICATION

Active listening is crucial. Whether you're in a lecture or engaging in a group discussion, make a conscious effort to focus on what is being said. Avoid interrupting, and try to understand the perspectives of your peers and professors. This not only demonstrates respect, but also fosters a positive learning environment.

Participate in class discussions. Sharing your thoughts not only helps solidify your understanding of the material, but also encourages open dialogue among your peers. Be confident, articulate your ideas clearly, and be open to feedback.

When working on group projects, establish clear communication channels. Define roles and expectations early on to avoid misunderstandings. Regular check-ins ensure that everyone is on the same page and that the project progresses smoothly. Use communication tools effectively, such as email and group messaging apps, to keep everyone informed and updated.

Outside the classroom, networking is a powerful tool. Attend seminars and workshops to connect with professionals and other students. Develop your elevator pitch, and practice introducing yourself concisely and confidently.

Embrace digital communication responsibly. Use professional language in emails, texts, and other online interactions. Remember that written communication lacks the nuance of face-to-face conversations, so choose your words carefully.

[58]
BASIC FINANCIAL LITERACY

College is where you'll start to assert your independence, both in terms of living on your own and managing your own money. Here are some key insights to help you understand basic financial literacy and avoid pitfalls that could jeopardize your future.

First, let's talk about budgeting. Create a realistic budget that includes your income and expenses. Be mindful of your spending habits, and prioritize essentials like tuition, housing, and food. It's easy to get carried away with discretionary spending, but overspending can lead to financial stress down the road.

While you probably won't have to start paying your student loans back until after you graduate, be sure you're using those funds as intended. If you look at your student loan as a windfall for personal use, you'll end up not having enough money to pay your tuition.

Credit cards can be a double-edged sword. While they offer convenience, misusing them can lead to high-interest debt. Use credit responsibly, pay your bills on time, and strive to maintain a good credit score — it'll help you buy large-ticket items in the future.

Emergency funds might not sound thrilling, but they're a financial lifesaver. Set aside money for unexpected expenses, such as flat tires or medical emergencies. Maintaining a safety net will prevent you from resorting to high-interest loans or maxing out your credit cards in times of need.

[59]
HOUSEHOLD MANAGEMENT

Living on your own for the first time is thrilling, but it can also be daunting, since you must learn to manage your household without your parents. Here are some practical tips to help you navigate this exciting new chapter of independence.

As we've mentioned, budgeting is an important part of managing your life. Create a realistic budget that covers all your essentials — rent, utilities, groceries, and those occasional midnight snacks.

Meal planning might sound tedious, but it's a game-changer. Plan your meals for the week, make a shopping list, and stick to it. Not only will this save you money, but it also ensures you're eating well-balanced meals.

Speaking of food — learn the art of grocery shopping. Choose generic brands, buy in bulk when possible, and take advantage of sales and discounts.

Clean as you go — this applies to both your living space and your dishes. Set aside a few minutes each day to tidy up and wash dishes; your future self will thank you.

Embrace the power of communication. If you're sharing a living space, establish clear expectations with your roommates. Open and honest communication is the key to a harmonious living environment.

[60]
ESSENTIAL "DIY"
SKILLS

As you settle into your new life away from home, it's crucial to pick up some essential DIY skills; they'll save you money and empower you to handle everyday challenges.

Mastering basic cooking skills is mandatory. Learning to cook a few simple, nutritious meals will not only keep you healthy, but also save you a ton of cash. Get comfortable with chopping, sautéing, and following a recipe—you'll thank yourself later.

Taking care of common household issues is another skill that will come in handy. Whether it's a leaky faucet, a clogged drain, or a blown fuse, knowing how to troubleshoot and make basic repairs will save you from unnecessary stress and expense. Keep a basic toolkit with essentials like a screwdriver, pliers, and a wrench.

Learning to sew on a button or mend a small tear might seem old-fashioned, but these are practical skills that can extend the life of your clothes and, thus, save you money. Familiarize yourself with basic sewing techniques and invest in a sewing kit.

If you have a vehicle, understanding basic car maintenance is vital for your safety and the longevity of your ride. Learn how to check and change the oil, replace a flat tire, and jump-start a car. Familiarize yourself with the location and function of essential components like the battery, brakes, and fluid reservoirs.

CHAPTER SEVEN: RELATIONSHIPS AND SOCIAL SKILLS

In this chapter, we're going to explore the art of forming genuine connections. We'll touch on communication strategies, the ABCs of healthy relationships, and practical tips for mastering the social scene. Get ready to navigate the college social landscape like a pro!

[61]
MAKING NEW FRIENDS

For the first time in a while, you might be going to a school where you don't know anyone. Making friends might seem daunting at first, but it's easier than you might think. Here are some tips to help you navigate this challenge.

Be Open-Minded. College is a melting pot of diverse personalities. Embrace it! Be open to meeting people from different backgrounds, majors, and interests. You'll be surprised by the friendships that blossom when you step outside your comfort zone.

Attend Events. Whether it's club fairs, sporting events, or campus activities, get out there! Attend events that align with your interests. Shared passions are excellent conversation starters and can lead to genuine connections.

Join Clubs and Organizations. Colleges offer a multitude of clubs and organizations. Find ones that align with your hobbies or career goals. Not only will you meet like-minded individuals, but you'll also have a blast doing what you love.

Use Social Media. Connect with your college community through social media platforms. Many universities have dedicated groups for incoming students. It's a great way to introduce yourself, ask questions, and find potential friends before even stepping foot on campus.

Be Approachable. Smile, make eye contact, and don't be afraid to strike up a conversation. Approachability goes a long way in making others feel comfortable reaching out to you.

Attend Orientation. Don't skip orientation events — they're specifically designed to help you make connections and get to know your fellow students.

[62]
NAVIGATING ROMANTIC RELATIONSHIPS

Navigating the waters of romantic relationships during your college years can be both thrilling and challenging. Here are some tips to help you sail smoothly through the highs and lows of love.

Communication is Key

Open and honest communication is the foundation of any successful relationship. Be transparent about your feelings, expectations, and concerns. It's crucial to express yourself and actively listen to your partner.

Time Management

College life is hectic, and between classes, exams, and social events, it's easy to neglect your relationship. Schedule quality time with your partner to ensure you stay connected amidst the chaos.

Set Boundaries

Establishing boundaries is vital. Understand each other's comfort zones regarding personal space, time alone, and socializing. Respect these boundaries to maintain a healthy and balanced relationship.

Individual Growth

College is a time for personal growth and self-discovery. Encourage each other to pursue individual passions and goals. A strong relationship supports personal development rather than hindering it.

Handle Conflicts Maturely

Disagreements are inevitable, but it's how you handle them that matters. Stay calm, avoid blame games, and focus on finding solutions together. Learning to resolve conflicts constructively will strengthen your bond.

Trust Your Instincts

Trust your gut feelings about the relationship. If something doesn't feel right, address it. Trust is crucial, and if doubts persist, have an open conversation with your partner to gain clarity.

Maintain Independence

While it's wonderful to be part of a couple, it's equally important to maintain your individual identity. Don't lose sight of your personal goals and dreams.

Celebrate Small Moments

Cherish the little moments of joy, and celebrate achievements together. Life is a journey, and having a supportive partner can make the ride more enjoyable.

[63]
DEALING WITH CONFLICT

Conflict is like a pop quiz—it happens when you least expect it and can throw you off balance. However, because mastering the art of conflict resolution is a skill that will serve you well throughout your college journey and beyond.

Stay Calm and Collected

When conflict arises, stay calm; reacting impulsively can escalate the situation. Instead, give yourself a moment to process and collect your thoughts before responding.

Listen First, Speak Second

Effective communication is a two-way street. Listen actively to understand the other person's perspective before expressing your own. This demonstrates respect and creates an open space for resolving differences.

Use "I" Statements

Frame your concerns using "I" statements to express your feelings and thoughts without sounding accusatory. For example, say "I feel overwhelmed when..." instead of "You always make me feel..."

Seek Understanding

Try to understand the other person's viewpoint. This doesn't mean you have to agree, but showing empathy fosters a more collaborative environment and opens the door to finding common ground.

Choose the Right Time and Place

Timing matters. Avoid addressing conflict in the heat of the moment, especially in public spaces.

Seek Mediation if Necessary

If the conflict persists, consider involving a neutral party or a trusted friend. They can offer a fresh perspective and help guide the conversation toward resolution.

Learn from Each Conflict

View conflicts as learning experiences. Reflect on what triggered the disagreement and how it can be handled differently in the future.

[64]
EFFECTIVE COMMUNICATION IN RELATIONSHIPS

You will develop different kinds of relationships throughout your college career, and your interactions with each person will be unique. However, one aspect of relationships that remains constant is communication.

Active Listening: Do you ever find your mind wandering during a conversation? Stop that! Practice active listening by fully engaging in what your partner is saying. Put down the phone, make eye contact, and respond with thoughtful comments.

Express Yourself: Don't keep your thoughts on lockdown—share your feelings and thoughts openly. Bottling up emotions leads to misunderstanding. If something's bothering you, let your partner in.

Non-Verbal Cues: Sometimes, words can't express it all. Pay attention to body language, facial expressions, and gestures. Understanding these cues enhances your comprehension and connection.

Be Mindful of Tone: Your tone can be a game-changer. Even the best words can be misunderstood if delivered with the wrong tone. Keep it respectful and considerate. Remember, it's not just what you say, but *how* you say it.

Apologize and Forgive: We're all human. Mistakes happen. Be quick to apologize when you're wrong, and don't hold grudges. It's a two-way street that keeps your relationship healthy.

Set Boundaries: College life is a whirlwind, and it's easy to get overwhelmed. Clearly communicate your boundaries and respect the other person's.

[65]
UNDERSTANDING CONSENT

If you haven't already, college presents the ideal time to equip yourself with the knowledge and understanding of consent. This isn't just a box to check off—it's a vital aspect of building healthy, respectful relationships that will shape your life in college and after.

Consent is all about communication and respect. It's not a one-time agreement but an ongoing and voluntary collaboration between all parties involved. Whether it's a romantic relationship, a casual encounter, or even a simple hug, ensuring everyone is on the same page is paramount.

Before we do anything else, let's debunk the myth that consent is only about saying "yes" or "no." While verbal communication is important, consent is also expressed through body language and non-verbal cues. Pay attention to your partner's comfort level, and be mindful of any signs that may indicate discomfort or hesitation.

Clear communication is your ally. Before engaging in any intimate activity, have an open and honest conversation about boundaries, desires, and expectations. It might feel a bit awkward at first, but it's much better than miscommunication down the road.

Remember, consent can be withdrawn at any moment. If someone changes their mind or feels uncomfortable, respect their decision without question. No means no, and respecting that builds trust and fosters a culture of empathy.

[66]
MANAGING LONG-DISTANCE RELATIONSHIPS

If you're already in a relationship as you head off to college but your partner is going to another school, you've found yourself in a long-distance relationship. It can be a challenging ride, but managing a long-distance relationship in college is totally doable with the right mindset and a bit of effort.

As always, communication is your lifeline. Make a schedule, set up regular video calls, and keep the conversation flowing. Be honest about your feelings, and encourage your partner to do the same.

Surprise them with a handwritten letter, care package, or visit if possible. These small gestures can make a huge impact, reminding your partner that you're thinking of them even amid the chaos of college.

Trust your partner and yourself. College is a time for personal growth, and it's important to have faith in your relationship. If you've got a solid foundation, a bit of distance won't shake it. Stay confident in your connection, and remember that trust goes both ways.

Now, let's talk about FOMO (Fear of Missing Out). It's real, especially in college, but don't let FOMO dictate your relationship. Embrace your college experience, make new friends, and explore opportunities without guilt. Trust your partner and yourself to maintain a healthy balance between social life and your relationship.

Of course, plan visits whenever possible. Whether it's a weekend trip or a holiday break, having something to look forward to can keep the flame burning. After all, creating shared experiences helps strengthen your bond.

[67]
DEVELOPING
EMPATHY

Empathy is the ability to understand and share the feelings of others, which serves as a cornerstone for building meaningful relationships, fostering effective communication, and navigating the diverse landscapes of college life. Here are some key principles to help you cultivate empathy during your college journey.

The first key is to practice active listening. In the hustle and bustle of academic life, it's easy to get caught up in your own thoughts and concerns. Put away distractions and engage in conversations with an open mind.

Next, seek out diverse experiences. College provides a unique opportunity to interact with individuals from all walks of life. Embrace this diversity, and actively engage with people whose experiences differ from your own.

The next step is to practice perspective-taking. Put yourself in others' shoes to understand their feelings and motivations. This involves stepping outside your own worldview and considering alternative viewpoints.

Finally, cultivate self-awareness. Understanding your own emotions and reactions is essential in developing empathy. Reflect on your own experiences, biases, and preconceptions. Recognizing and addressing your own emotions enables you to approach others with empathy.

[68]
CULTURAL
SENSITIVITY

Imagine your college campus as a microcosm of the world, with students from different countries, ethnicities, religions, and cultural backgrounds.

Each person brings a unique set of values, traditions, and perspectives to the table. Cultural sensitivity is the ability to recognize and appreciate these differences without judgment, fostering an inclusive environment where everyone feels valued and understood.

Why is this so important? First off, it enriches your own college experience. Engaging with diverse cultures exposes you to new ideas, traditions, and ways of thinking. It broadens your horizons, helping you become a well-rounded individual with a more comprehensive worldview.

Secondly, cultural sensitivity is a crucial aspect of effective communication and collaboration. As you navigate group projects, social events, and even casual conversations, understanding and respecting diverse perspectives will make you a more skilled communicator. This, in turn, enhances your ability to work effectively with people from different backgrounds, a skill that's highly sought after in today's globalized job market.

Moreover, in an era where cultural diversity is celebrated, demonstrating cultural sensitivity reflects positively on your character. It shows that you appreciate and respect the richness that diversity brings to the tapestry of human experience. Employers and graduate programs alike value individuals who can navigate and thrive in diverse environments.

[69]
BUILDING A
SUPPORT NETWORK

It can be scary to be without your established support system when you don't know anyone on campus. That's why it's important for you to begin building a new support network to ensure your well-being and success.

First, don't be afraid to step outside your comfort zone. Join clubs, organizations, and attend campus events that align with your interests. This is an excellent way to meet like-minded individuals who share your passions and hobbies. Whether it's a sports team, a cultural club, or an academic group, these communities can become your anchor in a sea of new faces.

Take advantage of orientation programs and welcome events. Colleges often organize these to help students integrate into the campus community. It's an opportunity to meet both new students and experienced upperclassmen who can offer valuable insights and guidance.

Use social media platforms to connect with your peers. Many colleges have dedicated groups or pages where students can introduce themselves, ask questions, and plan meet-ups. Engaging in these online communities can be a great icebreaker before meeting people in person.

Remember, everyone's in the same boat. Many students are looking to make connections, so don't hesitate to initiate conversations. Attend study groups, participate in class discussions, and be present in communal areas to increase your chances of meeting new people.

[70]
RECOGNIZING
UNHEALTHY RELATIONSHIPS

As we've demonstrated in this section, relationships are an essential part of personal growth and development, especially during your college years. While many connections can be enriching, it's important to recognize the signs of unhealthy relationships to ensure your well-being.

Pay attention to communication dynamics, and make sure you feel heard and valued in your interactions. If you find yourself in a situation where communication is characterized by constant misunderstandings, manipulation, or criticism, it may be a sign of an unhealthy relationship.

Another red flag is the lack of personal space and boundaries. Healthy relationships respect individual autonomy and personal boundaries. If you feel pressured to give up your personal time, hobbies, or friendships for the sake of a relationship, it may be a warning sign.

Keep an eye on power imbalances. A power dynamic in which one person consistently holds more control or influence can lead to an unhealthy and potentially toxic relationship. It's important to foster an environment where both partners feel empowered and valued.

Additionally, be aware of any signs of emotional or physical abuse. No relationship should involve fear, intimidation, or violence. If you ever feel unsafe or threatened, seek help immediately. College campuses often have resources like counseling services or support groups that can assist you in navigating challenging situations.

Overall, stay vigilant and prioritize your well-being by recognizing and addressing signs of unhealthy relationships. Surround yourself with positivity, and strive for connections that contribute to your personal and academic success.

CHAPTER EIGHT: TECHNOLOGY AND DIGITAL LITERACY

In this section, we'll explore the dynamic universe of technology and digital literacy. Our goal is to arm you with the critical skills needed to excel in today's tech-centric society. Let's get started!

[71]
UTILIZING ACADEMIC SOFTWARE

Academic software can either make your academic journey a breeze or a labyrinth of confusion. Fortunately, these tips will ensure that you're at the cutting edge of digital learning from your first day in class.

Before you do anything else, familiarize yourself with the software provided by your institution. Whether it's learning management systems like *Canvas* or *Blackboard*, collaboration tools such as *Google Workspace* or *Microsoft 365*, or subject-specific software, it's important to understand the basics. Dive into tutorials, or seek guidance from tech-savvy friends to ensure you're not left scratching your head when deadlines loom.

Efficiency is the name of the game. Leverage features like cloud storage, collaborative editing, and real-time feedback to streamline your workflow. Platforms like *Google Docs* or *Office 365* allow you to collaborate seamlessly on group projects, making the dreaded group project a tad more bearable.

Don't shy away from time-management tools. Academic software often comes equipped with calendars, task lists, and reminders. Sync these with your class schedule, assignment due dates, and exams to stay on top of your game.

Dive into the world of online resources. Many academic software suites offer supplementary materials, discussion forums, and interactive content. Explore these to enhance your understanding of course material and engage with peers.

Stay on top of software updates. Developers regularly roll out new features, bug fixes, and security patches. Make it a habit to keep your software updated to benefit from the latest enhancements and ensure a smooth user experience.

[72]
ONLINE SAFETY AND PRIVACY

As a college student, you'll be using the internet frequently. Here are some tips to ensure you don't inadvertently reveal too much when you're researching, shopping, or socializing online.

Fortify Your Passwords

Strengthen your defenses by creating robust passwords that have a mix of special characters and numbers. Avoid using easily-guessable information like birthdays or names. Change passwords regularly, and refrain from using the same password across multiple accounts.

Use Two-Factor Authentication (2FA)

Add an extra layer of security to your online presence by enabling 2FA whenever possible. This feature ensures that, even if your password is leaked, the hacker still needs a second key to get to your information.

Conceal Your Identity

Be mindful of what personal information you reveal online. Minimize the details you share on social media, and reassess privacy settings to control who gets to glimpse your world.

Update Your Software Regularly

Make it a habit to check for updates to your software and apps to ensure you have the most recent version available. These updates often include security patches that remove vulnerabilities, preventing hackers from exploiting weaknesses.

Be Wary of Phishing Attempts

Beware of deceptive emails and messages attempting to lure you into a trap. Verify the sender's legitimacy before clicking on any links or downloading attachments.

Arm Yourself with Virtual Private Networks (VPNs)

For a cloak of invisibility, consider using VPNs. They encrypt your online connection, making it challenging for prying eyes to decipher your digital footprints.

[73]
MASTERING DIGITAL COMMUNICATION

Whether you're shooting off emails to professors, participating in online discussions, or collaborating on group projects, effective communication is key. Here are some tips to help you ace the digital communication game.

Be Clear and Concise

When composing emails or messages, get straight to the point. Professors and peers appreciate clarity. State your purpose, ask your question, or share your thoughts concisely.

Professional Tone

While emojis and informal language are okay with friends, maintain a professional tone in academic communication. Address professors with respect, use proper salutations, and proofread your messages to catch grammar or spelling errors.

Timely Responses

Respond promptly to emails and messages. It shows that you're engaged and respectful of others' time. If you need more time to provide a detailed response, acknowledge the message quickly, and let them know when they can expect a more comprehensive reply.

Mind Your Digital Presence

Be mindful of your digital footprint, as colleges and employers often check social media profiles. Ensure your online presence aligns with the professional image you want to portray.

Participate Actively in Discussions

Engage actively in online discussions. Contribute thoughtfully, ask questions, and respond to your peers. This not only enhances your understanding of the material, but also fosters a sense of community in your virtual classroom.

Use Technology Wisely

Familiarize yourself with communication platforms, be it email, discussion forums, or collaborative tools. Stay updated on any new features or updates that can enhance your digital communication experience.

[74]
LEVERAGING SOCIAL MEDIA RESPONSIBLY

Social media can connect us, inform us, and entertain us; however, if you're not careful, it can also become a source of stress and distraction. Here are some tips to help you rock the social media game without it taking over your world.

Mindful Posting: Before hitting that 'post' button, think about the content you're sharing. Consider its impact on your personal and professional image. Remember, the internet has a long memory, and future employers might scroll through your social media profiles.

Privacy Settings are Your BFFs: Take the time to understand and tweak your privacy settings. Not everything needs to be visible to the entire world. Control who sees your posts, and be cautious about sharing personal information.

Time Management: Social media can be a major time-sucker. Set specific times for checking your accounts to avoid mindless scrolling that eats into your study or relaxation time.

Be Wary of FOMO: It's easy to feel like everyone is having the time of their lives while you're stuck in the library. Remember, people share their highlight reels on social media, so don't let FOMO get to you.

Digital Detox Days: Every now and then, take a break from the digital world. Spend a day without checking your feeds. This can do wonders for your mental health and help you stay focused on what truly matters.

Respect Others: Treat your online interactions with the same respect you would in person. Avoid spreading negativity, cyberbullying, or engaging in heated debates that can escalate quickly.

[75]
BASIC TROUBLESHOOTING SKILLS

In the digital age, having basic computer and technology troubleshooting skills is as crucial as remembering your class schedule. Whether you're dealing with a stubborn laptop, a finicky printer, or glitchy software, troubleshooting tech issues can save you from major headaches.

First off, the classic "turn it off and on again" trick is not just a meme—it works! Restarting your device can resolve a multitude of issues, from slow performance to unresponsive software. Give it a shot before delving into more complex solutions.

When it comes to connectivity problems, check your Wi-Fi settings and ensure you're connected to the right network. Sometimes, a simple reset of your router can do wonders. If you're still struggling, try "forgetting" the network and reconnecting.

Dealing with a frozen or crashing application? Task Manager (Ctrl + Shift + Esc on Windows or Command + Option + Esc on Mac) is your best friend. It lets you see what's hogging your system's resources and force-quit misbehaving programs.

Is your laptop getting too hot? Overheating can be a common issue. Clean out those dust bunnies from your vents, invest in a cooling pad, and consider adjusting power settings to keep things cool.

For those inevitable moments when your files disappear into the abyss, don't panic. Check the recycle bin or trash first; it might be a simple case of accidental deletion.

When it comes to software updates, don't procrastinate. Keeping your operating system and applications up to date can patch security vulnerabilities and improve overall performance.

[76]
UNDERSTANDING DATA SECURITY

Data security is a topic that may seem a bit dull, but it's crucial in our increasingly-digital world. You'll create and obtain a lot of data during your college years, and you need to know how to keep it all secure.

To begin with, think of your personal data as treasure. In the digital landscape, your treasure includes things like passwords, bank details, social media accounts, and even your course projects.

Start by fortifying your passwords. Make them strong and unique for each account, combining letters, numbers, and symbols. As mentioned earlier, always enable two-factor authentication to make sure your data requires two keys to access.

Be cautious about the apps and websites you use. Opt for trustworthy platforms, and keep your software updated. Regular updates help fix any weak points that hackers might exploit.

Avoid oversharing on social media. Broadcasting your every move is akin to putting up neon signs pointing to the location of your personal information. Be mindful of what you share, who you share it with, and review privacy settings to control who has access to your information.

Back up your data regularly. Imagine losing your term paper the night before it's due—not a pleasant thought, right? Create backups that can rescue your work from the clutches of unexpected digital disasters.

Stay vigilant against phishing attempts. If an email or message seems suspicious, don't click any links or provide personal information.

[77]
EXPLORING ONLINE LEARNING TOOLS

When you're juggling classes, assignments, and social life, the constant struggle for balance is no easy feat. Fortunately, the internet can help you succeed in finding that balance. Embrace the vast array of online tools at your disposal to make your life easier.

The backbone of academic success lies in organization. Use online planners like *Google Calendar* or *Todoist* to map out your schedule, assignments, and deadlines. Sync them across devices to stay on top of your game, making time management a breeze.

Collaboration is key, and tools like *Google Docs* and *Microsoft Teams* allow for seamless group projects. Real-time collaboration ensures everyone is on the same page, fostering teamwork and boosting productivity.

Leverage the power of communication platforms like *Slack* or *Discord* for effective group discussions and project coordination.

Online libraries such as *JSTOR*, *Google Scholar*, and your college's digital repository are treasure troves of academic articles and resources. Refine your research skills and save time by accessing a wealth of information at your fingertips.

Enhance your study sessions with apps like *Quizlet* for flashcards and *Anki* for spaced repetition. These tools optimize your memory retention, transforming your study routine into a strategic advantage.

When it comes time to edit, *Grammarly* and *Hemingway Editor* come to the rescue, polishing your prose and ensuring your papers are sharp and error-free.

Don't forget the importance of self-care. *Calm* and *Headspace* offer mindfulness and meditation exercises to combat stress, keeping your mental health in check.

[78]
DIGITAL ORGANIZATION TECHNIQUES

First things first: Embrace the power of folders. Your computer's desktop might currently resemble a chaotic warzone of files, but creating well-organized folders is like giving your digital space a makeover. Sort your documents by subject, semester, or project to make finding them a breeze.

Next up, let's talk about note-taking apps. Ditch the old-fashioned notebook and go digital. Apps like *OneNote*, *Evernote*, or *Google Keep* allow you to keep all your notes in one place, making it easy to access them anytime, anywhere.

Calendars are your new best friend. Use them, not just for class schedules, but also for deadlines, social events, and even self-care. Set reminders to ensure you never miss a beat. *Google Calendar* and *Microsoft Outlook* are popular choices, but find what works best for you.

Speaking of deadlines, task management apps are a lifesaver. *Trello*, *Asana*, or *Todoist* help you break down your projects into manageable tasks, making the workload seem less daunting. You can also set deadlines and track your progress — a surefire way to stay on top of your game.

Maybe most importantly of all, back up your work regularly. Cloud storage services like *Google Drive*, *Dropbox*, or *Microsoft OneDrive* ensure that your hard work is safe and accessible whenever you need it.

[79]
EMERGING TECH TRENDS IN EDUCATION

As you make your way through college, it will be essential to stay tuned into the ever-evolving landscape of education. Here are some emerging trends that could shape your college experience and beyond.

Personalized Learning: The one-size-fits-all approach to education is becoming a thing of the past. Personalized learning is gaining momentum, where educational content and methods are tailored to individual student needs and pace. Adaptive learning platforms, online resources, and data analytics are being leveraged to create a more customized learning experience.

Technology Integration: Brace yourselves for an increased integration of technology in education. Virtual and augmented reality, artificial intelligence, and online collaboration tools are reshaping traditional classroom settings. From interactive simulations to virtual study groups, technology is enhancing the learning process and preparing you for a tech-driven future.

Globalization of Education: The world is becoming more connected, and so is education. Expect an increase in opportunities for international collaboration, study abroad programs, and cross-cultural learning experiences. Embrace the chance to broaden your perspectives, interact with diverse cultures, and build a global network that extends beyond the borders of your campus.

Emphasis on Soft Skills: While your academic knowledge is crucial, the importance of soft skills like communication, critical thinking, and adaptability cannot be overstated. Take advantage of extracurricular activities, internships, and projects to develop these skills that will make you stand out in the professional world.

Lifelong Learning Mindset: The days of completing education and considering it a wrap are gone. The future demands a commitment to lifelong learning. Embrace the idea of continuous skill development, and be open to adapting to new technologies and industries throughout your career.

[80]
E-PORTFOLIO
DEVELOPMENT

This section will introduce you to an awesome tool that can elevate your academic and professional journey: the ePortfolio. Now, as you already know, college life can be overwhelming—assignments, exams, and the constant pressure to build a promising future. That's where the ePortfolio comes in handy as a game-changing asset.

Let's start at the very beginning. What's an ePortfolio? Think of it as your digital showcase, a personalized platform to exhibit your achievements, skills, and projects. It goes beyond the traditional resume, allowing you to present a comprehensive picture of who you are as a student and potential professional.

One key advantage of an ePortfolio is the ability to curate your best work. It's not just grades; it's showcasing projects, papers, and presentations that reflect your growth and expertise. This is your chance to demonstrate your skills in a tangible way, giving potential employers or graduate programs a deeper understanding of your capabilities.

Building your ePortfolio is like crafting your personal brand. Choose a clean and professional design that reflects your style. Highlight your academic achievements, but don't forget to include extracurricular activities, internships, and volunteer experiences. This holistic approach paints a vivid picture of your capabilities and interests.

Regularly update your ePortfolio to keep it relevant and aligned with your current goals. As you progress through college, add new projects, achievements, and skills. This not only showcases your continuous growth, but also ensures that your ePortfolio remains a dynamic representation of your evolving strengths.

CHAPTER NINE: HEALTH AND WELLNESS

When you're on your own for the first time in college, health and wellness might take a back seat to everything else that's captured your attention. However, you need to put them back in the forefront of your priorities. This chapter helps you do just that, giving you tips to stay healthy in both mind and body throughout your college experience.

[81]
HEALTHY EATING
ON CAMPUS

Let's talk about the dining hall or cafeteria first. It's your hub for meals, so make smart choices. Create a colorful plate by loading up on veggies and fruits. They're packed with essential vitamins and minerals to keep you energized. Balance your meals with lean proteins like grilled chicken or tofu and choose whole grains over refined ones for sustained energy.

Snacking is inevitable, but don't let it derail your health goals. Stock up on convenient, nutritious snacks like yogurt, nuts, and fresh fruit. Keep a stash in your dorm or backpack to resist the temptation of vending machines loaded with processed treats.

When you're on the go, think ahead. Pack a homemade sandwich with whole grain bread, lean protein, and veggies. It's a quick, cost-effective alternative to fast food. Carry a reusable water bottle to stay hydrated throughout the day and cut back on sugary drinks.

Don't forget about moderation! It's okay to indulge occasionally, but make it a treat, not a habit. Balance is key to a sustainable and enjoyable approach to eating well.

Of course, don't forget to prioritize sleep and manage stress. A well-rested and relaxed mind contributes to better food choices.

[82]
REGULAR
EXERCISE

Amid lectures, assignments, and social events, it's easy to sideline physical activity. However, incorporating exercise into your routine doesn't just help with building muscles or shedding a few pounds; it helps you cultivate a healthier lifestyle that can enhance your academic performance and general well-being.

One thing you'll find interesting as a college student is that regular exercise is proven to boost cognitive function. Engaging in physical activity increases blood flow to the brain, improving concentration, memory, and overall cognitive abilities.

Additionally, college life often comes with stress and anxiety. Exercise is a natural stress-reliever, releasing endorphins that act as your body's natural mood-lifters. It provides a valuable outlet for the stress accumulated from tight deadlines and demanding schedules. Instead of succumbing to the pressure, take a break to engage in activities like yoga, swimming, or a brisk walk to clear your mind and rejuvenate your spirit.

Consider incorporating short bursts of physical activity into your routine, such as taking the stairs instead of the elevator, walking or biking to class, or participating in quick home workouts. You don't need hours at the gym to reap the benefits—consistency is key.

Ultimately, prioritizing regular exercise is an investment in your overall well-being. It's not just about physical fitness; it's a holistic approach to leading a healthier, more balanced college life.

[83]
MENTAL HEALTH
AWARENESS

College life can be a rollercoaster of emotions, from the highs of new friendships and opportunities to the lows of academic stress and homesickness. As such, it's essential to pay attention and prioritize your mental well-being.

Understanding that mental health is as vital as physical health is the first step towards mental health awareness. Don't ignore those persistent feelings of sadness, anxiety, or stress. If you find yourself struggling to concentrate, feeling exhausted all the time, or withdrawing from activities you used to enjoy, it's time to take a pause and reflect.

Knowing when to seek professional help is crucial. Trust your instincts — if you feel overwhelmed or unable to cope, reach out to a mental health professional. Whether it's a counselor on campus, a therapist in the community, or a helpline, resources are available to support you.

Keep an eye out for warning signs, such as drastic changes in mood or behavior, extreme feelings of hopelessness, or thoughts of self-harm. Don't hesitate to talk to a friend or another trusted person in your life about what you're going through. Sometimes, just expressing your feelings can be a tremendous relief.

Remember, asking for help is a sign of strength, not weakness. Seeking professional assistance is a brave and responsible choice that shows you are taking control of your well-being. Colleges often have mental health services readily available, so take advantage of them.

[84]
SLEEP HYGIENE

First off, let's talk about consistency. Try sticking to a regular sleep schedule. We're not telling you to be a robot, but going to bed and waking up around the same time each day helps regulate your internal clock.

Make your sleep space cozy and comfortable. Invest in a decent mattress or pad, keep the room cool, and consider adding some blackout curtains to help relax your brain and body.

The blue light emitted by screens messes with your sleep hormones. Try shutting them down at least an hour before bedtime. Instead, grab a book or listen to some soothing tunes — your brain will thank you.

Let's not forget caffeine and midnight snacks. Whether it's coffee or cola, caffeine is often a staple of college life. Consider cutting off the caffeine supply several hours before bedtime. As much as you love that midnight snack, heavy meals can lead to a restless night. Choose something light if hunger strikes late.

Lastly, exercise — it's not just for gym buffs. A little physical activity during the day can do wonders for your sleep. It doesn't have to be a marathon; a stroll or some yoga will do the trick.

[85]
PRACTICING
SELF-CARE

Inevitably, you'll find yourself needing to recharge your mental batteries when you're in the middle of an intense semester. Here are some accessible self-care strategies to help you power through the challenges.

- **Nature Breaks:** Step outside and immerse yourself in nature, even if it's just for a short walk around campus or sitting in a nearby park. Fresh air and a change of scenery can do wonders for your mood and concentration.

- **Creative Expression:** Engage in activities that allow you to express yourself creatively. Whether it's doodling in the margins of your notebook, writing poetry, or playing an instrument, expressing your thoughts and feelings through art can be a therapeutic outlet.

- **Digital Detox:** Unplug from your devices for a designated period each day. Constant screen time can be draining, so take breaks from your phone and computer to give your eyes and mind a rest.

- **Gratitude Journaling:** Take a few minutes each day to jot down things you're grateful for. Focusing on positive aspects of your life, no matter how small, can shift your mindset and bring a sense of appreciation and contentment.

- **Laughter Yoga:** Laughter is a powerful stress-buster. You don't need a reason to laugh; simply practice laughter yoga exercises to boost your mood and release tension.

- **Power Naps:** While traditional sleep is essential, a quick power nap of 10-20 minutes can provide a mental refresh without interfering with your nighttime sleep schedule.

[86]
SUBSTANCE ABUSE AWARENESS

While most of your college career is going to be fulfilling and positive, it's vital to be aware of potential pitfalls that may hinder your success and well-being. One such concern is substance abuse, which can have severe consequences on your academic performance, mental health, and overall life satisfaction.

First and foremost, you must understand what substance abuse entails. Substance abuse refers to the harmful or hazardous use of psychoactive substances, including alcohol and illicit drugs—even prescription drugs can be abused. Recognizing whether you or someone you know is struggling with substance abuse is a critical step in addressing the issue.

One red flag is a noticeable change in behavior. If you or a friend has become increasingly withdrawn, irritable, or secretive, it might be indicative of a substance abuse problem. Frequent and unexplained mood swings, erratic behavior, or neglect of responsibilities are also warning signs.

Academic performance can serve as another indicator. If your grades are slipping, attendance is sporadic, or assignments are consistently incomplete, it's time to assess whether substance use is playing a role. Additionally, changes in physical appearance, such as sudden weight loss, changes in hygiene, or bloodshot eyes, may be signs of substance abuse.

Social relationships can also be affected. If you or someone you know is experiencing strained relationships with friends and family, or if there is a noticeable shift in social activities, it could be linked to substance abuse.

Acknowledging these signs is the first step toward seeking help. Don't hesitate to reach out to friends, family, or campus resources for support. Many colleges offer counseling services and confidential helplines to assist students facing substance abuse challenges.

[87]
SEXUAL HEALTH EDUCATION

While talking about sexual health may be uncomfortable, it's necessary, especially since sexual experiences might be new. It's important to prioritize your sexual health, now and for the rest of your life. Your well-being extends beyond textbooks and exams, and maintaining a healthy approach to relationships and intimacy is key.

Communication is your ally when it comes to healthy sexual relationships. Honest and open conversations with your partner(s) about boundaries, desires, and consent are non-negotiable. Mutual understanding creates a foundation for healthy relationships and ensures that everyone involved is on the same page.

Next, arm yourself with knowledge about contraception. There's no one-size-fits-all method, so explore your options and find what works best for you. Condoms, birth control pills, patches, and intrauterine devices (IUDs) are just a few choices. Remember, being informed empowers you to make responsible decisions about your sexual health.

Regular check-ups are like academic progress reports, but for your health. Schedule routine visits to a healthcare professional to stay on top of screenings for sexually transmitted infections (STIs) and other reproductive health concerns. Early detection can make a world of difference.

As we've mentioned, consent is the golden rule. Never underestimate its importance. It's not just a one-time agreement, but continuous communication throughout any intimate encounter. If it's not a clear and enthusiastic "yes," it's a *no*.

Don't forget to prioritize your mental and emotional health. College life can be stressful, and emotional well-being contributes significantly to your overall health. Seek support when needed, and remember that a healthy mind positively impacts all aspects of your life, including your sexual experiences.

[88]
NAVIGATING
HEALTH SERVICES

In the previous section, we mentioned getting regular checkups to make sure you're healthy. Taking care of your well-being as a college student is just as important as acing those exams and making lasting memories. Fortunately, most campuses offer health services to students, so let's look at what those services are and how to access them.

Before you need it, familiarize yourself with the campus health center. This is your go-to place for non-emergency medical care, vaccinations, and counseling services. Find out its location, operating hours, and the services provided. Many campuses offer routine check-ups, mental health support, and advice on nutrition and wellness.

Understanding your health insurance is vital. Whether you're covered under a school-sponsored plan or have your own, make sure you know the details. This knowledge will save you from unexpected expenses and help you take full advantage of your benefits.

As we've mentioned several times, don't hesitate to seek mental health support. College life can be stressful, and it's okay to ask for help.

In case of illness or injury, don't just push through it—visit the health center promptly. Early intervention can prevent minor issues from becoming major problems. Plus, your academic performance and overall experience will benefit from taking care of your health.

Whenever possible, be proactive about your well-being. Engage in campus wellness programs, join fitness classes, and stay informed about health-related events. Taking small steps towards a healthier lifestyle can contribute to your overall success during your college years.

[89]
MINDFULNESS AND MEDITATION

Your college journey will sometimes feel like a never-ending hustle, but there are secret weapons that can keep you centered and calm: mindfulness and meditation.

Imagine your mind as a bustling city, with thoughts zooming around like cars on a freeway. Meditation is your chance to hit the brakes and find a serene park within that city. It's not about stopping traffic, but rather *observing* it without getting caught up in the chaos.

College life will undoubtedly throw some curveballs your way, but mindfulness will help you take everything in stride, giving you a chance to step back, take a breath, and look at situations with clarity. When the pressure's on, meditation becomes your anchor, allowing you to successfully take on academic challenges and personal growth.

Beyond stress relief, mindfulness is a mental gym for focus. In a world full of distractions, your ability to concentrate is a golden ticket. Meditation trains your mind to stay present, helping you absorb information like a sponge and ace those exams.

Now, let's talk about your ultimate superpower—resilience. College is a rollercoaster of highs and lows, but meditation acts as your stabilizer. It teaches you to ride the ups and downs without losing your cool. When setbacks occur, you'll bounce back stronger, armed with the resilience to face whatever comes your way.

Moreover, mindfulness enhances your emotional intelligence, an asset in navigating relationships and collaboration. You can understand yourself and others on a deeper level, fostering a supportive and positive community.

[90]
BALANCING SCHOOL
AND HEALTH

The pressure in college is real, and the struggle to find equilibrium between academic demands and personal well-being can be a constant battle. However, in the end, it's a battle worth fighting.

Your health is your greatest asset. It's not just a cliché; it's a fact. We've already discussed the fact that adequate sleep, proper nutrition, and regular exercise will keep you level-headed and prepared to take on any challenge. These are the three pillars of balance, so pay attention to them.

Your mental health has also been addressed several times, but it's important enough to mention again. The stress and pressures of college might feel like a formidable foe, but taking breaks and giving your mind a breather is crucial. Don't underestimate the power of downtime; it's not a sign of weakness, but a strategic move to recharge your cognitive batteries.

Don't forget that social connections are your allies along your journey. Don't isolate yourself in the quest for academic glory; your friends will help ensure you maintain balance between school and health by getting you out from behind your books when you need to escape for a while.

Another tip we've mentioned before is time management. It's easy to get lost in the sea of assignments and deadlines, but waiting until the last minute only leads to added stress and missed opportunities. Remember to schedule time away from your studies and treat these appointments as importantly as anything else in your life.

CHAPTER TEN: TRANSITIONING TO POST-COLLEGE LIFE

Even as you begin your college career, you should look beyond the time you'll spend on campus to your life after graduation. The years will fly by, and suddenly, you'll find yourself accepting your degree and wondering what your next step will be.

[91]
ADJUSTING TO LIFE
AFTER COLLEGE

Before you know it, your time in college will come to an end when graduation day arrives. Adjusting to life after college can be both exhilarating and challenging, but with a few key considerations, you can navigate this transition smoothly.

To start, be patient with yourself. The post-college period is a time of self-discovery and adjustment. You may not have everything figured out immediately, and that's perfectly fine. Embrace the journey of learning and growth as you find your footing in the real world.

Networking is crucial during this phase. Your connections, both professional and personal, can open doors and provide valuable insights. Attend networking events, take advantage of social media, and stay connected with your college peers and professors.

Financial responsibility is another aspect to prioritize. Create a budget, understand your student loan obligations, and start saving for the future. Managing your finances early on will contribute to long-term stability.

Don't be afraid to explore different career paths. Your first job out of college may not be your dream job, and that's okay. Be open to diverse opportunities; continuous learning and adapting to new environments will serve you well in your professional journey.

Finally, prioritize self-care. The transition from college to the working world can be demanding, and it's crucial to maintain a healthy work-life balance. Take time for activities you enjoy, stay connected with friends and family, and prioritize your mental and physical well-being.

[92]
MANAGING
POST-GRADUATION
FINANCES

Once graduation day passes, you'll have to face the reality of your finances. While the prospect of financial independence may seem daunting, with some careful planning and discipline, you can set yourself up for a stable and prosperous future.

Take a close look at your student loans. Understand the terms, interest rates, and repayment options. Create a budget that allocates a portion of your income towards paying off these loans. Prioritize paying more than the minimum if you can, as it can significantly reduce the overall interest.

Building an emergency fund should be your next financial goal. Life is unpredictable, and having a financial safety net provides peace of mind when unexpected expenses arise. Aim to save at least three to six months' worth of living expenses in a separate account.

As you start your career, contribute to your employer-sponsored retirement plan, such as a 401(k) or equivalent. Taking advantage of employers' matching contributions is essentially netting you free money. The earlier you start investing, the more time your money has to grow through compound interest.

While it's natural to want to enjoy the fruits of your labor, consider maintaining a modest lifestyle, and continue living like a student for a little while longer. This approach will allow you to allocate more funds towards your financial goals, like paying off debts or saving for major life milestones.

Educate yourself about investing. Understand the different investment opportunities available, and don't shy away from seeking advice from financial professionals. Diversify your investments to mitigate risk and maximize potential returns over the long term.

[93]
NAVIGATING THE
JOB MARKET

Once you've graduated from college, you'll likely be expected to get a job and begin contributing to society. It can be an exciting time, but it's also quite intimidating, especially if you aren't sure what you want to do or you're having trouble finding a position in your field.

First and foremost, invest in self-discovery. Reflect on your strengths, passions, and values. Understanding yourself will enable you to make informed decisions about your career. Take advantage of career counseling services offered by your university to gain insights into potential career options and refine your goals.

Crafting a compelling resume and cover letter is essential. Tailor these documents to showcase your skills and experiences relevant to the job you're applying for. Use concrete examples to demonstrate your accomplishments and how they align with the requirements of the position.

Networking plays a crucial role in job hunting. Attend career fairs, industry events, and join professional networking platforms. Connect with alumni, professionals, and recruiters in your chosen field. Building relationships leads to valuable insights, mentorship, and job opportunities.

Stay informed about industry trends and developments. Subscribe to relevant newsletters, join online forums, and follow industry leaders on social media. This knowledge will not only make you a more informed candidate, but will also help you during interviews and networking conversations.

[94]
CONTINUING EDUCATION OPPORTUNITIES

As you step into the next chapter of your life, it's important to recognize the significance of continuing education beyond the confines of your college experience. The pursuit of knowledge is a lifelong endeavor, and there are numerous opportunities available to enhance your skills and stay competitive in today's dynamic job market.

One avenue to explore is professional certifications. These specialized credentials can provide a targeted and practical approach to acquiring specific skills relevant to your field. Many industries value certifications as a testament to your expertise, and earning them can significantly boost your employability.

Consider enrolling in workshops, seminars, and online courses. These short-term programs offer a flexible way to acquire new skills and deepen your understanding of specific subjects. Platforms like *Coursera*, *edX*, and *LinkedIn Learning* provide a plethora of courses taught by industry experts, allowing you to learn at your own pace.

Another option is pursuing a graduate degree. Advanced education not only allows for specialization in your chosen field, but also opens new opportunities for leadership roles. Many universities offer part-time or online graduate programs to accommodate working professionals, making it feasible to continue your education while gaining practical experience in your career.

[95]
RELOCATING FOR WORK OR STUDY

After spending between four and six years in college, you're probably excited to spread your wings by relocating for work or additional studies. Here are some valuable tips to ease your transition and make the most out of this journey.

Research and Plan Ahead: Before making any decisions, thoroughly research potential cities or universities. Consider factors like cost of living, job opportunities, cultural environment, and lifestyle.

Budget Wisely: Moving can be expensive, so create a detailed budget that includes moving costs, initial living expenses, and a safety net for unforeseen circumstances. Be realistic about your financial situation, and look for cost-effective ways to relocate.

Embrace Flexibility: Understand that relocating involves adapting to new environments. Be open to change and approach challenges with a flexible mindset.

Seek Housing Early: Start looking for accommodation well in advance to secure the best option within your budget. Consider factors like proximity to your prospective workplace or campus.

Stay Organized: Keep all important documents, such as academic transcripts, identification, and employment contracts, in a secure and easily-accessible folder. Being organized will save you time and stress during the relocation process.

Cultural Awareness: Familiarize yourself with the local culture and customs to facilitate a smoother integration. Respect and appreciation for diversity will help you build positive relationships with people from different backgrounds.

Self-Care: Relocating can be emotionally and physically demanding. Prioritize self-care to maintain your well-being. Establish routines that include exercise, healthy eating, and adequate sleep and leisure time.

Seek Out Local Services: Be proactive in seeking out local resources and support services, such as community groups or mentorship programs. Building a local support system will enhance your sense of belonging and ease the transition.

[96]
BUILDING A PROFESSIONAL NETWORK

If you've followed the advice in this book so far, you will have already developed a strong network of professors, peers, and alumni. As you step into the professional world, expanding your network to people outside your college world becomes a crucial aspect of your career development.

LinkedIn is Your Friend: Create a compelling *LinkedIn* profile that highlights your skills, experiences, and aspirations. Connect with alumni, industry professionals, and peers you've worked with during internships or class projects.

Attend Industry Events: Attend conferences, seminars, and workshops relevant to your field. These events provide excellent opportunities to meet professionals, learn about industry trends, and showcase your expertise.

Utilize Alumni Networks: Leverage your college's alumni network. Alumni are often willing to help recent graduates by offering guidance, mentorship, and even job referrals. Reach out to them through networking events organized by your alma mater or via *LinkedIn*.

Informational Interviews: Request informational interviews with professionals in your desired field. This is a great way to learn more about different career paths, gain insights into the industry, and establish meaningful connections.

Online Communities and Forums: Join industry-specific online forums and communities. Engage in discussions, share your knowledge, and seek advice from seasoned professionals.

Volunteer and Attend Meetups: Offer your time and skills by volunteering for relevant causes or joining professional organizations. Attend local meetups or networking events to interact with professionals in a more casual setting.

Professional Development Courses: Enroll in additional courses or obtain certifications to enhance your skills. These programs not only add value to your resume, but also provide opportunities to connect with like-minded individuals.

[97]
LIFELONG LEARNING STRATEGIES

Graduating from college doesn't mean learning is over. As you transition into the next phase of life, embracing a mindset of lifelong learning will prove invaluable. Here are some strategies to help you cultivate a commitment to continuous learning.

Curate a Reading Habit: Develop a reading routine that spans various genres and topics. Whether it's literature, non-fiction, or industry-related publications, reading broadens your perspective and enhances your knowledge base.

Embrace Online Courses and Workshops: The digital age has ushered in an era of accessible learning. Leverage online platforms such as *Coursera*, *edX*, or *LinkedIn Learning* to acquire new skills. These courses, often offered by prestigious institutions and industry experts, can enhance your qualifications and keep you updated on the latest trends in your field.

Networking and Mentorship: Surround yourself with individuals who inspire and challenge you. Engage in networking events, conferences, and seminars to connect with professionals in your industry. Seek out mentors who can guide you in your personal and professional growth.

Stay Tech-Savvy: The pace of technological advancement is relentless. To remain competitive, regularly update your digital skills. Familiarize yourself with emerging technologies, programming languages, and software relevant to your field.

Document Your Learning: Maintain a learning journal or portfolio to track your progress. This reflective practice helps solidify your understanding of new concepts and allows you to set goals for continuous improvement, serving as a tangible record of your commitment to lifelong learning.

Cultivate a Growth Mindset: Embrace challenges as opportunities to learn and grow. A growth mindset fosters resilience and a willingness to confront unfamiliar territory. Approach every experience as a chance to acquire new knowledge.

[98]
WORK-LIFE
BALANCE

We've already discussed establishing a study-life balance, and those tips will serve you well into your professional career. However, it can be even harder to maintain a work-life balance when you enter the workforce, because your financial and personal well-being depends on doing your job well. The good news is that you can learn to keep your work and personal lives in balance by using these strategies.

First, embrace the idea of micro-boundaries. Life is full of tiny moments, and so is your schedule. Instead of trying to divide your life into strict work hours and personal hours, integrate the two seamlessly. Find small, meaningful ways to blend the two worlds.

Consider the "80/20 rule," not just in your job, but in your personal life. Identify the 20% of activities that bring you 80% of your happiness, and focus on those. Apply this principle to your work tasks, relationships, and leisure activities.

Challenge the traditional notion of a 9-to-5 workday. The post-grad world isn't always structured that way, and your productivity might not align with conventional hours. Negotiate flexible working arrangements that suit your natural rhythm. Maybe you're more of a night owl or prefer a split shift. Be proactive in shaping your work hours to optimize your productivity and well-being.

Perhaps most important of all, don't underestimate the power of "no." Learn to decline tasks or commitments that don't align with your priorities. This doesn't mean you're selfish, just that you're protecting your time and energy for things that truly matter. Establishing boundaries early on will set the tone for a sustainable work-life balance post-graduation.

[99]
ALUMNI ENGAGEMENT

"Alumni engagement" is a term that you might not have heard yet, but it's about to become very relevant—it's a valuable resource that can shape your post-college journey.

Alumni engagement involves maintaining a connection with your alma mater, and it goes beyond the occasional nostalgic visit to campus. Staying engaged offers a myriad of benefits that extend far into your future. To start with, it's a networking goldmine! Your fellow alumni are spread across various industries, and maintaining those connections can open doors you never imagined.

This network can provide valuable insights, job opportunities, and mentorship. Many successful professionals are willing to guide recent grads, sharing their experiences and helping you navigate the early stages of your career.

Beyond the professional advantages, alumni engagement fosters a sense of community. Attend reunions, participate in alumni events, and make use of alumni directories to stay in touch. This network will not only help with career advancement; you'll form lasting friendships and connections that will enrich your personal and professional life.

Moreover, staying engaged allows you to give back. Whether it's through financial contributions, volunteering, or sharing your expertise, contributing to your alma mater strengthens the institution for future generations. Your success reflects positively on your alma mater, and your involvement can inspire and support the next wave of graduates.

Don't treat graduation as a farewell; consider it a new beginning, with your college playing a vital role in your ongoing journey. Stay connected, stay engaged, and watch how this network of support becomes an invaluable asset in your life.

[100]
PLANNING FOR
RETIREMENT EARLY

You may be wondering why we've included this section in a guide for college students. However, while retirement may seem like a distant concept, starting to save and invest early can significantly impact your financial well-being in the long run.

To begin your retirement plan, establish a budget that includes a dedicated portion for retirement savings. Take a realistic look at your income and expenses, allocating a specific percentage towards your retirement fund. The power of compounding interest works best when time is on your side, so the earlier you start, the more your money can grow over the years.

Take advantage of employer-sponsored retirement plans, such as 401(k)s. Many employers offer matching contributions, essentially providing free money towards your retirement savings. Maximize these opportunities by contributing at least enough to receive the full employer match, as it can significantly boost your overall retirement savings.

Diversification is another key principle in retirement planning. Instead of putting all your eggs in one basket, spread your investments across various asset classes to mitigate risks. A mix of stocks, bonds, and other investment vehicles can help create a balanced and resilient portfolio.

Stay informed about the different retirement savings options available, such as Individual Retirement Accounts (IRAs) and Roth IRAs. Each has its own advantages, and choosing the right one depends on your financial goals and tax considerations.

You're going to be tempted to wait to save for retirement until you're making enough money to feel like you can afford to put some aside. However, you should do everything you can to resist this temptation. The power of compounding, coupled with disciplined financial habits, can set you on a path towards a secure and comfortable retirement.

[101]
BE TRUE
TO YOURSELF

College is a time of self-discovery and growth, but that doesn't mean you have to do what everyone else is doing. Staying authentic to who you are will make this journey more fulfilling.

Don't feel pressured to conform to stereotypes or follow the crowd. College life often comes with certain expectations, but remember that everyone's journey is unique. It's okay if you don't find joy in stereotypical college activities like wild parties or staying up all night. Embrace what genuinely makes you happy, whether it's joining a club, exploring new hobbies, or simply spending quality time with like-minded individuals.

Take the time to understand your values and priorities. College offers a myriad of opportunities, but not every path is right for everyone. Reflect on your interests, and let those guide your choices. Whether it's choosing a major, joining a student organization, or deciding how to spend your weekend, make choices that align with your true self.

Don't be afraid to speak up and express your opinions. College is a place for diverse ideas and perspectives. Engage in meaningful conversations, challenge your beliefs, and be open to learning from others. Surround yourself with people who appreciate you for who you are and support your individuality.

Take care of your mental and physical well-being by setting realistic goals, prioritizing self-care, and knowing when to ask for help.

CONCLUSION

As you reach the final pages of this book, we want to commend you on the journey you've undertaken in pursuit of knowledge and personal growth. Your time in college has been a transformative chapter filled with challenges, triumphs, and a multitude of lessons that extend far beyond the confines of lecture halls and textbooks.

As you reflect on the wisdom shared within these pages, remember that the essence of your college experience lies not just in the pursuit of grades, but in the pursuit of self-discovery. You've navigated the intricate web of academia, balanced the demands of coursework, and built relationships that continue to enrich your life. The journey you've traveled has molded you into a more resilient, adaptable, and insightful individual.

One of the fundamental concepts shared throughout this guide is the importance of embracing change and uncertainty. Your college years have been a training ground for navigating the unpredictable twists and turns that life inevitably throws your way. Whether it was adjusting to a new living situation, overcoming academic challenges, or finding your place in the vast sea of extracurricular activities, you've honed the ability to adapt and thrive in diverse situations.

Now, as you stand on the threshold of graduation, gazing into the horizon of your future, it's crucial to acknowledge the skills and resilience you've cultivated during your time in college. The transition from the academic world to the professional one may seem like a daunting leap, but rest assured, you're well-equipped to face the challenges that lie ahead.

This guide has served as your compass, offering advice on academic success, personal development, and the nuances of the professional landscape. From crafting a compelling resume to acing job interviews, from managing workplace dynamics to maintaining a healthy work-life balance, these are the skills that will empower you as you tackle the professional world.

Remember, your education doesn't end here; it's a lifelong journey. The insatiable hunger for knowledge that drove you through countless late-night study sessions and numerous class discussions remains a powerful force. Cultivate a mindset of perpetual learning, stay curious, and remain open to the possibilities that each new experience presents.

Furthermore, cherish the relationships you've forged during your time in college. Your bonds with friends, mentors, and fellow students are invaluable treasures that will continue to shape and enrich your life.

The culmination of your college journey is not the end; rather, it's the beginning of a new chapter. You are armed with a wealth of experiences, skills, and a mindset that will position you for success in the vast landscape beyond academia. Embrace the uncertainties, celebrate your achievements, and continue to grow, evolve, and make a meaningful impact in the world.

Congratulations on reaching this milestone, and best of luck on the adventures that lie ahead!